THE ECONOMIC
VALUE OF
BIODIVERSITY

IUCN – THE WORLD CONSERVATION UNION

Founded in 1948, The World Conservation Union brings together States, government agencies and a diverse range of non-governmental organizations in a unique world partnership: over 800 members in all, spread across some 125 countries.

As a Union, IUCN seeks to influence, encourage and assist societies throughout the world to conserve the integrity and diversity of nature and to ensure that any use of natural resources is equitable and ecologically sustainable. A central secretariat coordinates the IUCN Programme and serves the Union membership, representing their views on the world stage and providing them with the strategies, services, scientific knowledge and technical support they need to achieve their goals. Through its six Commissions, IUCN draws together over 6000 expert volunteers in project teams and action groups, focusing in particular on species and biodiversity conservation and the management of habitats and natural resources. The Union has helped many countries to prepare National Conservation Strategies, and demonstrates the application of its knowledge through the field projects it supervises. Operations are increasingly decentralized and are carried forward by an expanding network of regional and country offices, located principally in developing countries.

The World Conservation Union builds on the strengths of its members, networks and partners to enhance their capacity and to support global alliances to safeguard natural resources at local, regional and global levels.

IUCN Communications Division
Rue Mauverney 28
CH-1196 Gland, Switzerland
Tel: ++ 41 22-000 00 01
Fax: ++ 41 22-999 00 10
E-mail: mail@hq.iucn.ch

IUCN Publications Services Unit
219c Huntingdon Road
Cambridge, CB3 0DL, UK
Tel: ++ 44 1223-277894
Fax: ++ 44 1223-277175
E-mail: iucn–psu@wcmc.org.uk

THE ECONOMIC VALUE OF BIODIVERSITY

DAVID PEARCE AND DOMINIC MORAN

IN ASSOCIATION WITH THE BIODIVERSITY PROGRAMME OF IUCN – THE WORLD CONSERVATION UNION

IUCN
The World Conservation Union

EARTHSCAN
Earthscan Publications Ltd, London

IUCN and CSERGE are grateful to the Government of Switzerland for its generous support in funding this project

First published in 1994 by
Earthscan Publications Limited
120 Pentonville Road, London N1 9JN
Email: earthinfo@earthscan.co.uk
World Wide Web: http://www.earthscan.co.uk

Reprinted 1995, 1997

A catalogue record for this book is available from the British Library

ISBN: 1 85383 195 6 paperback/1 85383 225 1 hardback

Typeset by DP Photosetting, Aylesbury, Bucks
Printed and bound by Biddles Ltd, Guildford and King's Lynn

Earthscan Publications Limited is an editorially independent subsidiary of Kogan Page Limited and publishes in association with the International Institute for Environment and Development and the World Wide Fund for Nature.

CONTENTS

LIST OF ILLUSTRATIONS

FIGURES

TABLES

viii · *The economic value of biodiversity*

NOTES ON THE AUTHORS

David Pearce is Professor of Economics at University College London and Director of the Centre for Social and Economic Research on the Global Environment (CSERGE), University College London and University of East Anglia, UK.

Dominic Moran is Research Fellow at the Centre for Social and Economic Research on the Global Environment (CSERGE), University College London.

PREFACE

This book began life as a report to the International Union for the Conservation of Nature (IUCN) (the World Conservation Union) in Gland, Switzerland, in 1993. IUCN is internationally renowned for its pioneering work on nature conservation. Jeff McNeely, IUCN's Chief Conservation Officer, has long shown an appreciation of the role that economics has to play in habitat and species conservation (see, for example, his own *Economics and Biological Diversity*, IUCN, Gland, 1988). Our original remit was to look just at the issue of *economic value*, ie the kinds of economic values that are generated by conservation activity but which may well not be captured in the market place. The result of this 'failure' to capture such economic values is a distortion, a tilted playing field with the odds stacked against conservation and in favour of the economic activities that destroy biological resources. In this book version of our report we have gone further and have asked *why biodiversity disappears* and how its economic value might be captured by various institutional mechanisms. The theme of the volume is therefore roughly as follows:

- economic forces drive much of the extinction of the world's biological resources and biological diversity; yet
- biodiversity has economic value. If the world's economies are rationally organized, this suggests that biodiversity must have less economic value than the economic activities giving rise to its loss;
- yet we know that many biological resources do have significant economic value. We also know that many of the destructive activities themselves have very low economic value; therefore
- something is wrong with the way actual economic decisions are made – for some reason they fail to 'capture' the economic values that can be identified;

● these 'economic failures' lie at the heart of any explanation for the loss of biological diversity. If we can address them, there is a chance of reducing biodiversity loss.

Our perspective is therefore peculiarly economic. We make no apologies for that. We do not imply that other disciplines are not relevant or not important. We focus on the economics because it is our area of expertise and because we believe, very strongly, that the 'economic paradigm' illuminates the debate over biodiversity loss.

Those familiar with our earlier books will detect the common theme. There is a strong and pervasive set of links between economy and environment. Failure to understand those links, complex though they often are, is a failure to understand the primary motive forces for environmental destruction. That failure carries through to the design of policies which have little real chance of making significant impacts on the loss of the world's environments. These themes are spelled out in detail in David Pearce, Anil Markandya and Edward Barbier, *Blueprint for a Green Economy* (1989); David Pearce, Edward Barbier and Anil Markandya, *Sustainable Development: Economics and the Environment in the Third World* (1990); David Pearce (editor), *Blueprint 2: Greening the World Economy* (1991); David Pearce (editor), *Blueprint 3: Measuring Sustainable Development*, (1993); David Pearce, *Economic Values and the Natural World* (1993), all published by Earthscan; and David Pearce and Jeremy Warford, *World Without End: Economics, Environment and Sustainable Development* (Oxford University Press, 1992).

Those seeking a guide to environmental economics can consult R Kerry Turner, David Pearce and Ian Bateman, *Environmental Economics: an Elementary Introduction* (Harvester Wheatsheaf, Hemel Hempstead, 1994).

David Pearce
and Dominic Moran
London, June 1994

ACKNOWLEDGEMENTS

We are very much indebted to Jeff McNeely of IUCN for constant encouragement to develop this book. A special word of thanks goes to Emily Fripp who helped prepare the original report for IUCN. Thanks also to all our colleagues in CSERGE, especially Kate Brown, Raffaello Cervigni, Kerry Turner, Neil Adger, Tim Swanson and Mike Norton-Griffiths for helping to develop the ideas and analyses from which we have borrowed freely.

Although the work was prepared for IUCN, we fully acknowledge the financial support of the UK Economic and Social Research Council (ESRC) without whose support for CSERGE's core programme on biodiversity we could not have functioned.

Special thanks to David Pearce's own stock of feline biological diversity – Blueprint, Floss and Dill – who continue to entertain.

1

INTRODUCTION

The loss of the world's biological diversity is causing major concern worldwide. That concern is embodied, for example, in the Convention on Biological Diversity negotiated at Rio de Janeiro in 1992. But how important is biodiversity? And how can priorities for conservation be determined? This volume is concerned with one important approach to these questions: the economic approach. The central argument is that by ascribing economic value to biodiversity, more powerful, more practical arguments can be formulated for its conservation. The book reviews the economic approach and the available evidence on the economic value of biodiversity

The term 'biological diversity', often shortened to 'biodiversity', is an umbrella term used to describe the number, variety and variability of living organisms in a given assemblage. Biodiversity therefore embraces the whole of 'Life on Earth'. Decline in biodiversity includes all those changes that have to do with reducing or simplifying biological heterogeneity, from individuals to regions. This is a more subtle definition than the global stock of *biological resources*, a more anthropocentric term for biota such as forests, wetlands and marine habitats. Biological resources are simply those components of biodiversity which maintain current or potential human uses. They represent the diversity about which most is known. This anthropocentric view of biological resources offers a convenient 'window' for economic analysis over alternative value paradigms such as 'intrinsic value': values in themselves and, nominally anyway, unrelated to human use. Intrinsic values are relevant to conservation decisions, but they are generally not measurable. As such they do not help to define actions in the context where choices have to be made against the backdrop of scarce conservation funds.

This chapter explains some of the key concepts of biodiversity and approaches to the measurement of biodiversity and its components. Some tentative estimates of rates of extinction are presented and qualified by a discussion of the scientific uncertainties which complicate these estimates and the choice of reliable indicators. Institutional and economic forces driving depletion are outlined prior to an introduction of the value categories relevant to biological resources. The chapter stresses the range of measures of diversity from different scientific perspectives. The different conceptualizations of biodiversity lead to different policy prescriptions, and require different indicators for monitoring and assessment.

THE MEANING OF BIOLOGICAL DIVERSITY

Biodiversity may be described in terms of genes, species, and ecosystems, corresponding to three fundamental and hierarchically-related levels of biological organization.

Genetic diversity

Genetic diversity is the sum of genetic information contained in the genes of individuals of plants, animals and micro-organisms. Each species is the repository of an immense amount of genetic information. The number of genes range from about 1000 in bacteria, up to 400000 or more in many flowering plants. Each species is made up of many organisms, and virtually no two members of the same species are genetically identical. This means for example that even if an endangered species is saved from extinction, it will probably have lost much of its internal diversity. When the populations are allowed to expand again, they will be more genetically uniform than their ancestral populations. For example, the bison herds of today are biologically not the same in terms of their genetic diversity as the bison herds of the early 18th century (McClenagham et al, 1990).

Population geneticists have developed mathematical formulae to express a genetically effective population size. These explain the genetic effects on populations which have passed through a 'bottleneck' of a small population size, such as the North American bison or African cheetah (WCMC, 1992). The resultant inbreeding may have a number of detrimental effects such as lowered fertility and increased susceptibility to disease. This is termed 'inbreeding depression'. The effects of small population size depend on the breeding system of the species and the duration of the bottleneck. If the bottleneck lasts for many generations, or population recovery is very slow, a great deal of variation can be lost. The converse, 'outbreeding depression', occurs when species become genetically differentiated across their range, and then individuals from different parts of the range breed.

Genetic differentiation within species occurs as a result of either sexual reproduction, in which genetic differences from individuals may be combined in their offspring to produce new combinations of genes, or from mutations which cause changes in the DNA.

The significance of genetic diversity is often highlighted with reference to global agriculture and food security. This stresses the reliance of the majority of the world's human population on a small number of staple food species, which in turn rely on supply of genes from their wild relatives to supply new characteristics, for example to improve resistance to pests and diseases (Cooper et al, 1992).

Species diversity

Species are regarded as populations within which gene flow occurs under natural conditions. Within a species, all normal individuals are capable of breeding with the other individuals of the opposite sex belonging to the same species, or at least they are capable of being genetically linked with them through chains of other breeding individuals. By definition, members of one species do not breed freely with members of other species. Although this definition works well for many animal and plant species, it is more difficult to delineate species in populations where hybridization, or self-fertilization or parthenogenesis occur. Arbitrary divisions must be made, and indeed this is an area where scientists often disagree.

New species may be established through the process of *polyploidy*, the multiplication of the number of gene-bearing chromosomes, or more commonly, as a result of geographic speciation. This is the process by which isolated populations diverge by evolution as a result of being subjected to different environmental conditions. Over a long period of time, differences between populations may become great enough to reduce interbreeding and eventually populations may be able to co-exist as newly formed, separate species. Within the hierarchical system used by scientists to classify organisms, species represent the lowest rung on this ladder of classification. In descending order, the main categories, or taxa, of living things are:

Kingdom
Phylum
Class
Order
Family
Genus
Species

We do not know the true number of species on earth, *even to the nearest order of magnitude*. Wilson (1988) estimates that the absolute number of species falls between 5 and 30 million, although some scientists have put forward even higher estimates, up to 50 million. At present approximately 1.4 million living species of all kinds of organisms have been described. The best catalogued groups include vertebrates and flowering plants, with other groups relatively under-researched, such as lichens, bacteria, fungi and roundworms. Likewise, some habitats are better researched than others, and coral reefs, deep ocean floor and tropical soils are not well studied. This lack of knowledge has considerable implications for the economics of biodiversity conservation, particularly in defining priorities for cost-effective conservation interventions.

The single most obvious pattern in the global distribution of species is that overall species richness increases with decreasing latitude. Not only does this apply as a general rule, it also holds within the great majority of higher taxa, at order level or higher. However, this overall pattern masks a large number of minor trends. Species richness in particular taxonomic groups, or in particular habitats, may show no significant latitudinal variation, or may actually decrease with decreasing latitudes. In addition, in terrestrial ecosystems, diversity generally decreases with increasing altitude. This phenomenon is most apparent at extremes of altitude, with the highest regions at all latitudes having very low species diversity (although these areas also tend to be of limited size, which may be one factor resulting in lower species numbers). In terms of marine systems, depth is the analogue of altitude in terrestrial systems and biodiversity tends to be negatively correlated with depth. Gradients and changes in species richness are also noticeably correlated to precipitation, nutrient levels and salinity, as well as other climatic variations and available energy.

Ecosystem diversity

Ecosystem diversity relates to the variety of habitats, biotic communities and ecological processes in the biosphere as well as the diversity within ecosystems. Diversity can be described at a number of different levels and scales:

- Functional diversity is the relative abundance of functionally different kinds of organisms.
- Community diversity is the number sizes and spatial distribution of communities, and is sometimes referred to as patchiness.
- Landscape diversity is the diversity of scales of patchiness.

No simple relationship exists between the diversity of an ecosystem and ecological processes such as productivity, hydrology, and soil generation. Neither does diversity correlate neatly with ecosystem stability, its resistance to disturbance and its speed of recovery. There is no simple relationship within any ecosystem between a change in its diversity and the resulting change in the system's processes. For example, the loss of a species from a particular area or region (local extinction or extirpation) may have little or no effect on net primary productivity if competitors take its place in the community. The converse may be true in other cases. For example, if herbivores such as zebra and wildebeest are removed from the African savanna, net primary productivity of the ecosystem decreases.

Despite these anomalies, Reid and Miller (1989) suggest six general rules of ecosystem dynamics which link environmental changes, biodiversity and ecosystem processes.

1 The mix of species making up communities and ecosystems changes continually.
2 Species diversity increases as environmental heterogeneity or the patchiness of a habitat does, but increasing patchiness does not necessarily result in increased species richness.
3 Habitat patchiness influences not only the composition of species in an ecosystem, but also the interactions among species.

4 Periodic disturbances play an important role in creating the patchy environments that foster high species richness. They help to keep an array of habitat patches in various successional states.
5 Both size and isolation of habitat patches can influence species richness, as can the extent of the transition zones between habitats. These transitional zones, or 'ecotones', support species which would not occur in continuous habitats. In temperate zones, ecotones are often more species rich than continuous habitats, although the reverse may be true in tropical forests.
6 Certain species have disproportionate influences on the characteristics of an ecosystem. These include *keystone species*, whose loss would transform or undermine the ecological processes or fundamentally change the species composition of the community.

The discussion has shown how biodiversity is a very complex and all-embracing concept, which can be interpreted and analysed on a number of levels and scales. The next section examines some approaches to measuring these concepts.

MEASUREMENT OF BIODIVERSITY

A better understanding of biodiversity can be obtained when we examine exactly what we measure in order to assess biological diversity. However, this also serves to highlight further the range of interpretations, and the importance placed on different hierarchical levels of biodiversity by scholars of different disciplines, and by policy makers. Reid *et al* (1992) have commented that there is even now no clear consensus about how biodiversity should be measured. Indeed, debates on the measurement of biodiversity have filled a substantial part of the ecological literature since the 1950s. This lack of consensus also has important implications for the economics of biodiversity conservation. At its most basic level, any measure of cost-effectiveness used to guide investments in conservation must have some index or set of indices of biodiversity change. In the following sections, some aspects of measurement of biodiversity are examined, distinguishing the same components of biodiversity: genetic diversity, species diversity and ecosystem diversity.

Measurement of genetic diversity

The analysis and conceptualization of differences within and among populations is in principle identical regardless of whether we are considering a 'population' to be a local collection of individuals, geographical race, subspecies, species, or higher taxonomic group. Genetic differences can be measured in terms of phenotypic traits, allelic frequencies or DNA sequences.

Phenetic diversity

Phenetic diversity is based on measures of phenotypes, individuals which share the same characteristics. This method avoids examination of the underlying allelic structure. It is usually concerned with measurement of the variance of a particular trait, and often involves readily measurable morphological and physiological characteristics. Phenetic traits can be easily measured, and their ecological or practical utility is either obvious or can be readily inferred. However, their genetic basis is often difficult to assess, and standardized comparisons are difficult when populations or taxa are measured for qualitatively different traits.

Allelic diversity

The same gene can exist in a number of variants and these variants are called alleles. Measures of allelic diversity require knowledge of the allelic composition at individual loci. This information is generally obtained using protein electrophoresis, which analyses the migration of enzymes under the influence of electric field. Allelic diversity may be measured at the individual level, or at the population level. In general, the more alleles, the more equitable their frequencies, and the more loci that are polymorphic, the greater the genetic diversity. Average expected heterozygosity (the probability that two alleles sampled at random will be different) is commonly used as an overall measure. A number of different indices and coefficients can be applied to the measurements to assess genetic distance (see Antonovic, 1990). The detection of allelic variation by electrophoresis has the advantage that it can be precisely quantified to provide comparative measures of genetic variation. However, the disadvantages are that it may not be representative of variation in the genome as a whole, and does not take account of functional significance or selective importance of particular alleles.

Sequence variation

A portion of DNA is sequenced using the polymerase chain reaction technique (PCR). This technique means that only a very small amount of material, perhaps one cell, is required to obtain the DNA sequence data, so that only a drop of blood or single hair is required as a sample. Closely related species may share 95 per cent or more of their nuclear DNA sequences, implying a great similarity in the overall genetic information.

Measurement of species diversity

Species diversity is a function of the distribution and abundance of species. Often, species richness – the number of species within a region or given area – is used almost synonymously with species diversity. However, technically, species diversity includes some consideration of evenness of species abundances. Let us first consider species richness as a proxy measure of species diversity.

In its ideal form, species richness would consist of a complete catalogue of all species occurring in the area under consideration, but this is not usually possible unless it is a very small area. Species richness measures in practice, therefore, tend to be based on samples. Such samples consist of a complete catalogue of all organisms within a taxa found in a particular area, or of a measure of species density in a given sample plot, or a numerical species richness defined as the number of species per specified number of individuals or biomass.

A more informative measure of diversity would also incorporate the 'relatedness' of the species in a fauna (Williams et al, 1991; Reid et al, 1992). Using a measure of species richness would imply that a region containing many closely related species would be preferred to one containing a fractionally smaller number of distantly related or genealogically unrelated species. Alternative measures being developed augment species richness with measures of the degree of genealogical difference. Derived from cladistic methods, these measures include the weighting of close-to-root species, higher-taxon richness, spanning-tree length and taxonomic dispersion (Williams et al, 1991). Close-to-root species and higher-taxon richness explicitly use polarity from the root of the cladogram to weight higher-ranking taxa or 'relic' species as distinct survivors of long-independent lineages and original conduits of genetic information. In contrast, spanning tree length and taxonomic dispersion are more general tree measures of sub-tree 'representativeness'. Polarity from the root of the tree is less important than the amount of the cladogram represented by a fauna or the choice of a fauna to evenly cover the diversity of subgroups found in the cladogram. There is considerable disagreement as to which measure best characterizes the pattern of difference in the popular concept of biodiversity, although there is considerable support for taxonomic dispersion as a method of selecting faunas which most evenly represent a variety of cladogram sub-groups. For the time being, difficulties in actual implementation of cladistic measures suggest reliance on cruder indicators of richness of genera or families for rapid assessment of species diversity.

Measurement of community diversity

Many environmentalists and ecologists put emphasis on con-servation of biodiversity at the community level. There are a number of factors which make measurement and assessment of diversity at this level more nebulous and less clearly defined. Many different 'units' of diversity are involved at the supra-species level, including the pattern of habitats in the community, relative abun-dance of species, age structure of populations, patterns of com-munities on the landscape, trophic structure, and patch dynamics. At these levels, unambiguous boundaries delineating units of bio-diversity do not exist. By conserving biodiversity at the ecosystem level, not only are the constituent species preserved, but also the ecosystem functions and services protected. These include pollu-tant cycling, nutrient cycling, climate control, as well as non-consumptive recreation, scientific and aesthetic values (see for example, Norton and Ulanowicz, 1992).

Given the complexities of defining biodiversity at community or ecosystem level already described, there is a range of different approaches to measuring ecosystem diversity. As Reid et al (1992) explain, any number of community attributes are components of biodiversity and may deserve monitoring for specific objectives. There are several generic measures of community level diversity. These include biogeographical realms or provinces, based on the distribution of species, and ecoregions or ecozones, based on physical attributes such as soils and climate. These definitions may differ according to scale. For example, the world has been divided into biogeographical provinces, or more fine-grained classifications which may be more useful for policy-making. More policy orientated measures include the definition of 'hotspots', based on the number of endemic species, and 'megadiversity' states.

These concepts will be discussed in the context of using indicators for assessing and monitoring biodiversity. The following section introduces extinction, and some of the estimates of current rates of species extinction which have resulted in urgent need for conservation of global biodiversity.

THE RATE OF BIODIVERSITY LOSS

Estimates of precise rates of loss of biological diversity are hampered by the absence of any baseline measurement. However, from evidence of island habitats it seems likely that the expansion of the human niche by various forms of conversion is geometrically related to extinctions. Further recent evidence from observation of potential 'indicator' species such as amphibians and birds provides some indication of accelerated loss in excess of historical or background rates (Pechmann et al, 1991; Myers 1993). Table 1.1 shows some estimates of current rates of species extinction based on extrapolations of human land use trends related to species area curves which are the basis of island biogeography. Over the next century the projected loss of species might be expected to be as high as 20 to 50 per cent of the world's totals which represents a rate between 1000 to 10000 times the historical rate of extinction (Wilson, 1988). The rate of loss is outstripping the natural regenerative capacity of evolution to throw up new or evolved species. The extinction 'outputs' far exceed the speciation

Table 1.1 *Estimates of the current rates of species extinction*

Estimate of loss of species (%)	Basis	Source
33–50 by year 2000	Forest area loss	Lovejoy (1980)
50 by year 2000	Forest area loss	Ehrlich (1981)
25–30 in 21st century	Forest area loss	Myers (1989)
33 in 21st century	Forest area loss	Simberloff (1986)

'inputs' (Ehrlich and Ehrlich, 1992). The potential effects of accelerated extinction and depletion of the genetic base may be discerned over varying time horizons. In the long term, processes of natural selection and evolution may be dependent on a diminished resource base, simply because fewer species are being born. The implications of species depletion for the integrity of many vital ecosystems are far from clear. The possible existence of depletion thresholds, associated system collapse, and huge discontinuities in related social cost functions, are potentially the worst outcome in any reasonable human time horizon. Such scenarios are indicative of the links between ecosystem integrity and economic well-being. More immediately, the impoverishment of biological resources in many countries might also be regarded as an antecedent to a decline in community or cultural diversity, indices of which are provided in diet, medicine, language and social structure (Harmon, 1992).

At least four questions emerge from the scientific uncertainty surrounding species loss.

1 What is the number of species from which to measure current rates of loss and the detection of this rate, allowing for background evolutionary turn-over?
2 How sound are the principals and predictions of island biogeography and by how much are current extinction estimates (probably) understated?
3 Given the likely time horizons at issue, can we be concerned with the perversion of the evolutionary processes as opposed to the immediacy of system thresholds and flips?
4 What is the potential for using indicator species or a more sophisticated index to guide conservation efforts, and is there any scientific consensus on appropriate species or ecosystems to be used?

The need to pursue cost-effective investment interventions in biodiversity conservation has added considerable urgency to these issues, and the indicators debate in particular. Reliance on pivotal key-stone or umbrella species (Noss et al, 1992) is appealing but crude. Similarly focusing on wider taxonomic groups or ecosystem functions provides few indications of the likelihood of successful interventions, given wider socio-economic pressures on wilderness ecosystems and protected areas. Criteria such as species sensitivity to habitat disruption or poor reproductive capacity can be combined with other socio-economic data such as population density, deforestation or figures on conservation investment expenditure, to provide some indication of where species are threatened. However, assuming some consensus definition of threat raises the issue of whether funding is most effectively directed to those areas most under threat, or away from them entirely in favour of areas with a higher likelihood of success. This in turn implies some objective assessment of a 'successful' intervention. Given that no species can be saved indefinitely, the objective decision criterion becomes the extra cost of an increment to the probability of survival (Montgomery et al 1994; Hohl and Tisdell, 1993).

Understandably the development of investment criteria designed to maximize diversity per dollar and incorporating a composite threat indicator is likely to take time. Inevitable data restrictions are certain to further complicate what is already a contentious exercise. Nevertheless, two facts are clear. At some point a consensus measurement of biodiversity is required to guide the investment of scarce funds. The resulting index may seem arbitrary and will inevitably contravene some section of scientific opinion but will be necessary to provide a general direction for biodiversity investment. Moreover, using this index, any cost-effective system of area triage will necessarily require some consideration of complementarity of resulting faunal designations. In other words, the selection of successive areas for protection, ideally needs to be based on the incremental complement to diversity afforded by the last fauna until the complement is reduced to zero (Vane-Wright et al, 1991; Faith, 1994). This is clearly a massive undertaking, requiring precise taxonomic inventories and as much socio-economic information as dictated by the guiding index. At the same time such a process could show how an excessive concentration on certain biota can yield diminishing returns. The process of building on rapid appraisal rules of thumb such as hot spot or mega-diverse areas has already begun (see Dinerstein and Wikramanayake, 1993; Pearce et al, 1994). Emerging prescriptions are considerably less discriminating than the precise genealogical indices outlined in this chapter, and do not as yet attempt any faunal complementarity ranking. They do, nevertheless, attempt to combine basic species richness indicators with the socio-economic parameters most immediate to biodiversity loss.

STRUCTURE OF THE BOOK

The following chapters take this largely scientific review as a point of departure for understanding the loss of biological diversity. Chapter 2 introduces core themes of fundamental causation and economic value and explains how these help to clarify some of the policy issues relevant to the biodiversity conservation debate. Chapter 3 sets the issue in the context of cost-benefit analysis. Chapter 4 looks at the causes of biodiversity loss. Chapter 5 summarizes the methodologies for economically valuing environmental resources. Chapter 6 summarizes the empirical literature on those values. Chapter 7 investigates the other side of the conservation issue – the economic value of the development alternative. Chapter 8 explores the issue of emerging global markets for biological resource conservation. Chapter 9 draws the various issues together.

2

SAVING BIODIVERSITY: AN OVERVIEW OF CAUSAL FACTORS

In summer 1992 in Rio de Janeiro, the world's nations agreed a global Convention on Biological Diversity. It aims to protect the world's biological resources from further erosion or, at least, to slow that rate of erosion down. Yet the rate of erosion of biodiversity is increasing. Despite the Convention, the need to demonstrate the importance of conservation remains as strong as it ever was, perhaps stronger. One aspect of the process of changing government and popular perceptions about biological resources is to show that the sustainable use of biodiversity has positive economic value, and that this economic value will often be higher than the value of alternative resource uses which threaten biodiversity. Subsequent chapters are concerned with three fundamental characteristics of the biodiversity debate:

1 *demonstrating the economic values of biological resources* in the contexts where the values are often not reflected in market processes;
2 explaining why, despite those economic values, *biodiversity continues to be threatened*;
3 finding ways to *capture or realize economic value*.

Recognition of a broader total economic valuation of natural assets can be instrumental in altering decisions about their use, particularly in investment and land-use decisions which present a clear choice between destruction or conservation. Such decisions are being faced in both developed and developing countries, where a host of competing social and economic claims increasingly conflict with the resource demands of area protection. Greater understanding of the functioning of natural ecosystems combined with enhanced valuation techniques are an increasing influence on national conservation strategies, while international and multilateral initiatives emphasize the global dimension to the issue of biodiversity loss. We argue that addressing the economic causes of biodiversity loss is extremely important if the world really does want to slow down the erosion of its biological resources. Much of the biodiversity that needs saving resides in the developing world. Since biodiversity conservation is not, understandably, a priority for the developing world, the resources needed for conservation must come from the North, while the political commitment must come from the South and North alike. However we would like the world to be, the brute fact is that only policies which offer mutual self-interested gains to both North and South stand a chance of succeeding. In the longer term we may hope for changes of attitudes and priorities in the world generally, especially as incomes rise in the South. But relying on such changes to bring about conservation is foolhardy and counterproductive. That is why the economic approach matters. It does emphasize mutual economic gain as the foundation for the solution to the biodiversity problem.

The main reason for the erosion of biodiversity is that there is an underlying disparity between the private and social costs and benefits of biodiversity use and conservation (Dixon and Sherman, 1990; Perrings and Pearce, 1992). Private costs and benefits refer to those losses and gains as perceived by the immediate user of the environment: the farmer, the industrialist, the consumer. Social costs and benefits refer to the losses and gains that accrue to society as a whole. Social and private interests often do not coincide: what is good for me as an individual may impose costs on the rest of society – so-called 'externalities'. Sometimes, as we will show, what is good for the world as a whole is also good for me as an individual, but no institutions exist for me to capture this 'global value'. So, from the perspective of the individual (the farmer, the industrialist, the fisherman etc) it pays to destroy biodiversity. But from the point of view of society as a whole, it often pays to seek ways of sustainably utilizing that biodiversity and, on many occasions, it pays to protect it in some outright fashion. 'Society' in this respect can be the local society, the nation, or the world as a whole.

Why do private and social interests diverge ? Chapter 4 looks at this issue in detail, but we summarize the main factors here:

- Freely functioning markets are based on narrow self-interest. The upstream polluter has no incentive to account for the costs he imposes on a downstream user of the river. This is *market failure* and what is happening is that the downstream *externality* – the third party cost – is being ignored by the upstream polluter. Note that the failure arises from the free functioning of the market place. The economic approach should not be confused with any advocacy of free markets. However, as we shall see, functioning markets that are controlled in a particular way are powerful weapons for biodiversity conservation.
- Governments have a habit of intervening in markets. They may do this with the best of intentions. Indeed, they often intervene to remove the main elements of the externality caused by market behaviour. This is exactly what environmental regulation does. But, unfortunately, a great many other interventions are contrary to the interests of the environment, even where those interventions appear to serve some social purpose. Notable examples include activities to give financial incentives for deforestation, the underpricing of water resources, agricultural protection, and so on. There is therefore *intervention failure*. Note also that this failure can 'co-exist' with market failure: they are not exclusive.
- Many conservation activities yield *global benefits*. If biodiversity is conserved in a tropical forest, for example, it yields a benefit to people in other countries, either because they simply want it to be there, or because it helps sustain basic biogeochemical cycles on which human survival depends. But if the country in question receives no financial or other resources to pay for these *global external benefits*, it will have no incentive to look after the biological resources. There is another form of market failure which we will call *global appropriation failure*. Note that this failure arises not from the functioning of markets, but from the fact that the markets are not there at all. They are *missing markets*. Moreover, as we show in Chapter 4, global missing markets can be present with local market failure and with intervention failure. When they are combined in this way they do much to explain why biodiversity disappears.

But how are we to demonstrate that these 'failures' are important? They might, after all, be trivial when compared to the urgent need to change land uses for the benefit of economic development. The issue of *biodiversity resource valuation* is therefore a key issue in investment decisions about land use. Although the most sophisticated approaches are still largely restricted to developed country studies, those conducted elsewhere are increasingly demonstrating the magnitude and potential returns possible from sustainable use of biodiversity (SUB). The benefits of SUB should not be exaggerated; some wild claims have been made for the economic value of plant-based pharmaceuticals, eco-tourism and so on. Nonetheless, it is important to tease out what these values might be, and to explain why they are not being more widely realized.

THE PROXIMATE CAUSES OF BIODIVERSITY LOSS

We distinguish between the proximate causes and the fundamental causes of biodiversity loss. Proximate causes show up as the more popular explanations of biodiversity loss: eg logging, agricultural clearance of forested land, pollution. Fundamental causes lie behind these proximate causes and are rooted in economic, institutional and social factors. The main proximate cause of loss is *land conversion*, ie the conversion from one land use to another, where

Table 2.1 *Conversion of natural habitat to agriculture*

	1900 million hectares pa cropland	1980 million hectares pa cropland	% change
Developing			
Sub-S Africa	73	222	+204
Latin America	33	142	+330
South Asia	89	210	+136
China	89	134	+51
South-east Asia	15	55	+267
Developed			
North America	133	203	+53
Europe	145	137	−5
(ex) USSR	147	233	+58

Source: International Institute for Environment and Development and World Resources Institute (1987)

Table 2.2 *Recent rates of conversion to specialized agriculture*

Conversion to cropland: Increase in area under crops 1977/9–1987/9 (%)			Conversion to pastureland: Increase in area under permanent pasture 1977/9–1987/9 (%)		
1	Suriname	53	1	Korea Rep.	116
2	Paraguay	47	2	Ecuador	44
3	Burkina Faso	28	3	Paraguay	33
4	Thailand	22	4	Canada	27
5	C d'Ivoire	21	5	Thailand	27
6	Uganda	20	6	Costa Rica	24
7	Mongolia	19	7	Philippines	23
8	Guinea Bissau	18	8	Vietnam	21
9	Brazil	17			
10	Rwanda	17			

Source: World Resources Institute and International Institute for Environment and Development (1992)

land use includes sustainable management systems or even doing nothing with the land at all (wilderness). Table 2.1 shows some rates of conversion of natural habitats to agriculture.

High rates of conversion have clear implications for biodiversity loss. Of special concern are rates of conversion in the so-called megadiverse states: areas identified as being of high species endemism. Table 2.2 shows historical conversion rates to specialized agriculture.

THE ECONOMIC VALUATION OF ENVIRONMENTAL GOODS

A common taxonomy for environmental asset valuation is presented in Table 2.3. Conceptually, total economic value (TEV) of an environmental resource consists of its use value (UV) and non-use value (NUV). A use value is much as it sounds – a value arising from an actual use made of a given resource. This might be the use of a forest for timber, or of a wetland for recreation or fishing, and so on. Use values are further divided into direct use values (DUV), which refer to actual uses such as fishing, timber extraction etc; indirect use values (IUV), which refer to the benefits deriving from ecosystem functions such as a forest's function in protecting the watershed; and option values (OV), which is a value approximating an individual's willingness to pay to safeguard an

Table 2.3 *Categories of economic values attributed to environmental assets*

	Use values	Total economic value	Non-use values	
Direct use	*Indirect use*	*Option values*	*Bequest values*	*Existence values*
Outputs directly consumable	Functional benefits	Future direct and indirect values	Use and Non-use value of environmental legacy	Value from knowledge of continued existence
Food, Biomass, Recreation, Health	Flood control, Storm protection, Nutrient cycles	Biodiversity, Conserved habitats	Habitats, prevention of irreversible change	Habitats, Species, Genetic, Ecosystem

asset for the option of using it at a future date. This is like an insurance value.

Non-use values (NUV) are slightly more problematic in definition and estimation, but are usually divided between a bequest value (BV) and an existence or 'passive' use value (XV) (see Arrow et al, 1993). The former measures the benefit accruing to any individual from the knowledge that others might benefit from a resource in future. The latter are unrelated to current use or option values, deriving simply from the existence of any particular asset. An individual's concern to protect, say, the blue whale although he or she has never seen one and is never likely to, could be an example of existence value (see for example Randall and Stoll, 1983). Thus in total we have:

$$TEV = UV + NUV = (DUV + IUV + OV) + (XV + BV)$$

A sizeable literature has built up around the application of valuation techniques to a range of biological resources (see Chapter 6). As an example, Table 2.4 shows a set of identified functions of forests. Although not indicating the value category of each function, it is fairly clear where most belong, and also the extent of overlap in valuation. Thus direct use of timber and an indirect watershed protection function are often mutually exclusive, and double counting should therefore be avoided.

How useful the TEV classification is in practice is debatable.

Table 2.4 *Environmental functions of forests*

Sources of materials and services	Sink for wastes	General and life support
Timber	Absorption of waste	Genetic pool
Fuelwood	Recycling nutrients	Climate regulation
Other business products	Watershed protection	Carbon fixing
Non-wood products	Protecting soil quality and	Habitat for people, flora and
Agricultural production	erosion resistance	fauna
Recreation and tourism		Aesthetic, cultural and
		spiritual source
		Scientific data

Existing valuation techniques can distinguish use values from 'non-use' values, but attempts to isolate option, bequest and existence value are more problematic. Following recent legislative and legal controversies in the US and Australia, the concept of existence or 'passive' use values has recently come under considerable scrutiny (Rosenthal and Nelson, 1992; NOAA 1992; Desvousges et al, 1993).

The claim that existence value in some sense represent 'counter-preferential' values, motivated by moral concern, obligation or altruism, clearly poses problems for the conventional definition of an economic value. However, by taking the purpose of benefit measurement to be one of demonstrating economic value, however it is motivated, many of these problems disappear. Nonetheless, it is as well to be aware that the underlying principles and procedures for economic valuation are still debated.

IS TOTAL ECONOMIC VALUE REALLY TOTAL?

It is tempting to think that economists have captured all there is to know about economic value in the concept of TEV. But this is obviously not correct. First, recall that they are not claiming to have captured *all* values, merely economic values. Second, many ecologists say that total economic value is still not the whole economic story. There are some underlying functions of ecological systems which are prior to the ecological functions that we have been discussing (watershed protection and so on). Turner (1992) calls them 'primary values'. They are essentially the system characteristics upon which all ecological functions are contingent. There cannot be a watershed protection function but for the underlying value of the system as a whole. There is, in some sense, a 'glue' that holds everything together, and that glue has economic value. If this is true, then there is a total value to an ecosystem or ecological process which exceeds the sum of the values of the individual functions.

The discussion suggests three reasons why biological diversity is important.

1 The first reason is based on the concept of economic value. If biodiversity is economically important we would expect this to show up in *expressed willingness to pay for its conservation*. Shortly, we will show that this is indeed the case.

2 Economic value measurement will understate 'true' economic value because of the probable failure to measure *primary life support functions*. This kind of economic value is difficult to observe because it is unlikely to be recognized until some disastrous event has happened: landslides consequent upon deforestation, loss of fishing grounds due to pollution, and so on.

3 Economic value does not capture – nor is it designed to capture – *intrinsic value*.

3

CONSERVATION VERSUS DEVELOPMENT

THE COSTS AND BENEFITS OF LAND USE CONVERSION

The individual's view

Land use conversion is the primary factor explaining biodiversity loss. It is essential, then, to understand why land use conversion takes place. We begin with a stylized situation: a rational economic agent deciding whether to conserve or develop the land he owns or rents. To 'fix' the context we might assume that the decision in question is whether to conserve an area of tropical forest or to develop it, say by clearing it for agriculture. Economic rationality suggests that this decision will be determined by the relative profitability, or *rate of return*, of the two options. Within the conservation option we include *sustainable use* of the forest for, say, agro-forestry or for non-timber products such as medicinal plants, eco-tourism etc. Note that the relevant rates of return are those that accrue to the land owner or tenant. At this point no account is taken of any returns to society or to the world as a whole.

In this simplified situation, then, the decision to conserve or use sustainably will be the right one if:

Rate of return from SUB > Rate of return from 'Development'

where SUB is the 'sustainable use of biological diversity', ie the conservation option. This can be written:

$$B(SUB) - C(SUB) > B(DEV) - C(DEV) \qquad (1)$$

or

$$B(SUB) - C(SUB) - [B(DEV) - C(DEV)] > 0 \qquad (2)$$

where

B(SUB)	=	the benefits of sustainable use of the forest;
B(DEV)	=	the benefits of traditional development of the land for, say, agriculture or forestry or industry;
C(SUB)	=	the costs of the sustainable use option;
C(DEV)	=	the costs of the development option.

Rule 1 or 2 simply says that the net benefits from sustainable use of biodiversity should exceed the net benefits from development if conservation is to be preferred to development. Recall that the benefits and costs here are all defined in terms of the returns to the individual. They are *private costs and benefits.*

One complication that needs to be addressed immediately is the relevance of time. Typically, the land owner will prefer benefits now rather than later, and costs later rather than now. To allow for this we have to introduce *discounting.* Discounting permits us to compare gains and losses that occur over different time periods. The simplest way to approach it is to imagine the choice of $1 now or $1 next year. From the individual's standpoint there are several reasons why the $1 is preferred now. First, the $1 now could be invested (in a bank or in land or other assets) to become $1 plus accrued interest next year. If the interest rate is r, then the $1 now is worth $(1+r) next year. So the comparison of $1 now and $1 next year becomes a comparison of $1 next year and $(1+r) next year. Clearly, the $(1+r) is preferred, which is the same as saying that $1 now is preferred. Another way of putting this is that $1 next year is worth $1/(1+r) now. This sum is the *present value* of the future flow of income, the factor 1/(1+r) is the *discount factor* and r is the *discount rate.* Note that on this analysis the discount rate can be found by seeing what rate of return can be earned by investing money. This is known as the *opportunity cost of capital* approach to discounting. But there are other reasons for discounting. First, the individual may simply be impatient, even if he or she knows that they will be alive next year and even if they know the $1 will certainly be there next year. This impatience motive is called *pure time preference* discounting. As it happens, this time preference may be reinforced by the fact that the individual is not certain of being alive in the following year. There will be some discounting to reflect mortality risk. This is usually regarded as being part of pure time preference. A second factor is that the individual may expect to be richer next year anyway, so that $1 of additional income next year does not appear to be quite so important as $1 now. This is *discounting due to diminishing marginal utility of income*, where 'utility' here is simply the economist's term for individual welfare or well-being, and 'marginal' means 'extra'. So this form of discounting simply reflects the expectation that an extra (marginal) $1 next year is worth less in utility terms than an extra $1 now. The resulting discount rate that emerges from these considerations, s, is known as the *social time preference rate*. The rates s and r tend to differ in the real world and there is a debate as to which one should be used. For our purposes we need to note only that, from the individual's standpoint, both s and r are positive, ie $s > 0$ and $r > 0$.

Allowing for time, rule (2) needs to be restated in terms of *present values* to be:

$$PV[B(SUB) - C(SUB)] - PV[B(DEV) - C(DEV)] > 0 \quad (3)$$

where $PV(B) = \Sigma\ B_t/(1+r)^t$, or $\Sigma\ B_t/(1+s)^t$, and similarly for costs.

Equation (3) already gives us an insight to what is happening with land use conversion. If the value of SUB is low and that for DEV is high, then, other things being equal, land conversion will take place. Very simply, from the standpoint of the individual, it is more profitable to 'develop' than to conserve. Now, if the benefits of SUB accrue in unmarketed form – ie there is no obvious market for them – then the individual landowner has no incentive to take account of them. They may, for example, accrue to other people, even other people in some other country (like existence value). The benefits from development are 'real' and tangible. The benefits from SUB are often intangible. Put another way, the rate of return from conservation will appear to be very low, even zero, to the landowner or tenant.

The effect of discounting is a little more complex but worth exploring. A great many land conversions, especially those that relate to tropical forests, result in unsustainable land uses. Thus, a forest area may be cleared through burning. The burning converts the nutrient matter in the forest biomass into ash which then acts as a fertilizer for the nutrient-weak forest soil. The fire also acts as a pesticide. Crops are then grown and these use up much of the stock of nutrients in the soil. So, what was a renewable resource system becomes a non-renewable resource system: the living forest is replaced by a 'mine' of nutrients. As the nutrient value of the soil declines, so the land user reaps lower and lower returns from staying on the land. He eventually moves on and clears the next area of land. Left alone, new forest might be generated. But other users may come into the area, say a rancher with cattle. These cattle then use up the remaining store of nutrients in the soil and then the land may become truly degraded, ie unsuited to any agricultural use and with low prospect of regenerating forest.

The alternative to forest clearance is sustainable use of the land. If it is truly sustainable (some such allegedly sustainable uses themselves damage the forest), then that use can last for a very long time. This suggests that it should be preferable to the returns to 'nutrient mining' discussed above, since that ends when the soil is truly depleted. *But the problem is that discounting can make the non-sustainable use preferable to the sustainable use.* Figure 3.1 shows why this might be so. Because the future benefits from sustainable use are discounted, they may appear to matter little to the land owner, whereas the immediate benefits of conversion are higher, even though they result in zero long-term benefits. Of course, if the land-owner knows there is some further forest area he can colonize once the existing one is depleted, this adds to the incentive to deforest.

Figure 3.1 (a) shows the hypothetical 'cash flows' for non-sustainable nutrient mining and for sustainable land use. Nutrient mining has the higher short-term profits but zero long-term profits. Sustainable land use has long-term profits but lower immediate returns. Figure 3.1 (b) shows the effect of discounting. Both lines 'bend downwards'. The present values are the areas under these curves. If the heavy shaded area is greater than the hatched area, then the non-sustainable use is preferred.

Thus, two factors already provide some insight into why deforestation – and hence biodiversity loss – appears to be 'economically rational' from the individual's standpoint. First, the returns from clearance may simply be higher than the returns from conservation because the latter may consist of non-market benefits or benefits that accrue to people other than the landowner. Second, the effect of discounting is to discriminate against sustainable uses of the land if those uses have lower *initial* returns, even though the returns last much longer.

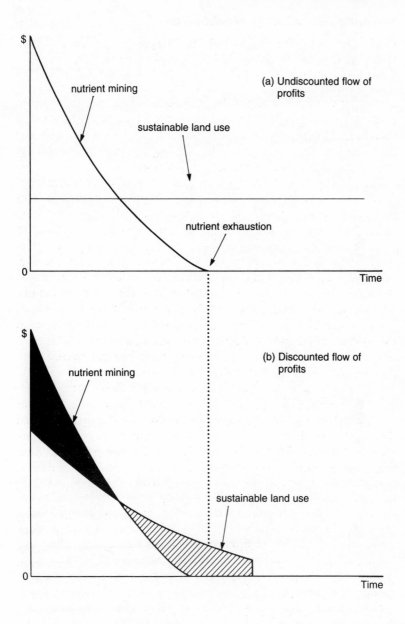

Figure 3.1 *Discounting and sustainable land use*

Society's view and the world view

The analysis so far has looked at land conversion from the individual's standpoint. What of society's view? From the social standpoint we need to redefine the benefits and costs in equation (3). We also need to ask if society's discount rate is the same as that of the individual.

As Chapter 2 showed, the benefits of conserving biodiversity are divided typically into use values and non-use values. Together, use and non-use values make up the total economic value of biodiversity conservation.

The second adjustment arises from the fact that, as noted above, both use and non-use values can reside in the host nation or globally (where globally means all nations other than the host nation). Using 'n' to denote national and 'g' to denote global, and using the TEV notation from Chapter 1, we can now write:

$$TEV(SUB) = UV + NUV = DUV + IUV + OV + BV + XV$$
$$(4)$$

and

$$TEV(SUB) = UV_n + UV_g + OV_n + OV_g + BV_n + BV_g + XV_n + XV_g$$
$$(5)$$

The expression for the cost-benefit rule, then, is that sustainable use will be preferred if:

$$PV\ [TEV(SUB) - C(SUB)] - PV[B(DEV) - C(DEV)] > 0\ (6)$$

Equation (6) sets the requirements for the comparison of sustainable land use and its opportunity cost, namely the forgone development values. It indicates what would be needed for sustainable use to be preferred over traditional development land use if a national host country standpoint is taken, and if that country seeks to secure the biggest gains in national efficiency. It tells us that conservation is preferred if the *national* gains are greater than the costs, and that those national gains will be larger still if the country can 'capture' some of the global use and non-use values. Once again, if the individual land user does not get part of the national gains from conservation, or part of the global gains, then he has no incentive to act in accordance with equation (6). He will simply operate according to his own private gains and losses.

This divergence between social, global and private returns does much to explain why biodiversity is being reduced. Chapter 4 takes the analysis further.

MEASURING BENEFITS AND COSTS

Equations (3) and (6) are the fundamental equations needed to establish *why* biodiversity loss occurs. If social, global and private costs and benefits diverge then there will be a strong incentive to convert land. This is market failure in both the local and global sense of Chapter 2. As we shall see in Chapter 4, government intervention actually makes the situation worse because it often exaggerates the private returns from destroying biodiversity.

The rates of return are measured in terms of economic benefits and economic costs. These costs and benefits have specific definitions in economics. Benefits and costs reflect either *willingness to pay* (WTP) to secure a gain (or benefit) or to avoid damage (a cost); or *willingness to accept* (WTA) compensation to forgo a gain or tolerate a cost. These WTP and WTA measures in turn reflect individuals' preferences which are the 'raw material' of economic valuation. If, for some reason, it is thought right to reject individual preferences as the basis for resource allocation, then the economic efficiency criterion will not be appropriate. Table 3.1 summarizes the relevant linkages.

Whereas it was traditionally thought that WTP and WTA would not diverge very much, recent evidence suggests that they can, and do. Typically, WTA may be a magnitude several times that of WTP, a difference unaccounted for by the limits set by income on WTP and which limit is not present for WTA. Differences are explained mainly in terms of (a) loss aversion, ie valuations of

Table 3.1 *The sources of economic value*

Gains	Losses
Preference for securing a benefit = = >	Preferences against losses = = >
Willingness to pay for a benefit or	Willingness to pay to avoid a loss or
Willingness to accept compensation to forgo the benefit	Willingness to accept compensation to tolerate a loss

damages (a loss) are higher than the comparable gain relative to some initial endowment of assets, including environmental assets; and (b) limited substitutes for environmental goods (Kahneman and Tversky, 1979; Knetsch and Sinden, 1984; Knetsch, 1989; Hanemann, 1991). The relevance of the WTP/WTA distinction is that it will matter which measure is used when comparing the rates of return to alternative land uses. This issue is considered further when appraising the evidence of different rates of return. In the meantime, Table 3.2 illustrates the degree of divergence found between WTA and WTP in valuation studies.

ECONOMIC VALUES AND MORAL ISSUES

Many people feel it is quite wrong to allow economic values to play any role in determining what should and should not be 'saved' by way of conservation. For the implication of equation (6) is that if the total economic value of conservation using a WTP metric does *not* prove to be greater than the value of development, then development 'should' take place. They would argue that conservation is a moral issue, to be determined by some discussion of the 'rights' of other species, the rights of indigenous peoples and other minorities, and by our moral obligations to future generations. Status of biodiversity is an end in itself rather than an instrumental means to an end. If the economic approach puts conditions on absolute or permanent protection then such rights are contravened and the paradigm is unacceptable.

The idea that the 'moral' view is opposed to the 'economic' view rests on many confusions. First, the economic view is itself a moral view – it takes what is effectively a *utilitarian* approach to conservation. What the critics are complaining of is not so much the economics as the underlying philosophy of normative economics, *utilitarianism*. Of course, it is quite proper for such a philosophical debate to take place. The problem is that, in the absence of 'meta-ethical' principles, principles that enable us to choose between apparently competing philosophies, the debate risks being rather sterile *from the standpoint of getting things done*. Put another way, the moral debate has gone on for a very long time and is as relevant to, say, crime and punishment as it is to biodiversity conservation. The fact that such debates have not been resolved is not surprising, but, of course, that in turn cannot be a reason for not continuing to try

Table 3.2 The divergence between willingness to pay and willingness to accept (US$)

Study and entitlement	Means			Medians		
	WTP	WTA	Ratio	WTP	WTA	Ratio
Hypothetical surveys:						
Hammack and Brown (1974): marshes	$245	$1044	4.2			
Sinclair (1978): fishing	35	100	2.9			
Banford et al (1979)	43	120	2.8			
Fishing Pier				47	129	2.7
Postal Service	22	93	4.2	22	106	4.8
Bishop and Heberlein (1970): goose hunting permits	21	101	4.8			
Rowan et al (1980): visibility	1.33	3.49	2.6			
Brookshire et al (1980): elk hunting*	54	143	2.6			
Heberlein and Bishop (1985): deer hunting	31	516	16.5			
Real exchange experiments:						
Knetsch and Sinden (1984): lottery tickets	1.28	5.18	4.0			
Heberlein and Bishop (1985): deer hunting	25	172	6.9	1.33	3.40	2.6
Coursey et al (1987): taste of sucrose octa-acetate#	3.45	4.17	6.9			
Brookshire and Coursey (1987): park trees##	10.12	417	1.4	1.35	12.96	2.1

Source: Kahneman, Knetsch and Thaler (1990)
* Middle-level several used in study
# Final values after multiple iterations
Average of two levels of tree plantings

and resolve it. The problem is that much conservation policy to date has been based on non-utilitarian approaches. Yet by many accounts the current situation is one of crisis. It would seem fair, then, to choose between the competing philosophies according to their potential for saving biodiversity in real world contexts. We argue that this favours the economic-utilitarian approach.

Alternative moral standpoints would also be more tenable if they confronted the real world context of making choices. If all biological resources have 'rights' to existence then presumably it is not possible to choose between the extinction of one set of them rather than another. All losses become morally wrong. But biodiversity loss proceeds apace for the reasons we have cited and for one other we have not so far mentioned: the competition between mankind and other species for the available space. The reality is that little can be done to prevent huge increases in the world's population – it is in that respect 'too late' for a good deal of the world's biological diversity. If so, it is essential to choose between different areas of policy intervention – not everything can be saved. This view is reinforced by the fact that the world is extremely unlikely to devote major resources to biodiversity conservation. We can argue that it should, but we know it will not. The issue then becomes one of using the existing budgets as wisely as possible. If not everything can be saved then a *ranking* procedure is required. And such a ranking is not consistent with arguing that everything has a right to exist.

Moreover, if we are right, and economic 'causes' are very important, then, presumably, the moral view would sanction the correction of the economic factors giving rise to excess biodiversity loss. That would be a start at least. In other words, whatever moral standpoint is taken it does not affect the design of a practical agenda for conservation, and that agenda should begin with the economic factors.

Finally, even if some do not like the economic-utilitarian approach, it has a major function which is not served by any other approach to conservation. It explains why biodiversity is being lost. It tells us that, since people very often *are* utilitarian in their decisions about land use and conservation, a utilitarian approach is needed in order to understand the process of loss, and hence the process of policy correction.

4

THE CAUSES OF BIODIVERSITY LOSS

ECONOMIC FAILURE

Chapters 2 and 3 introduced the idea of 'economic failure': the inability of existing markets to capture the 'true' value of natural resources. Two sources of such failure were identified:

1 *Market failure* – distortions due to the 'missing markets' in the external benefits generated by biodiversity conservation; and
2 *Intervention or government failure* – distortions due to government actions in intervening in the workings of the market place.

Within market failure we distinguished *local market failure* and *global market failure*. The former relates to the inability of markets to capture some of the local, national benefits of biodiversity conservation. Or, looked at from the standpoint of land conversion, local market failure refers to the failure of markets to account for the external costs of biodiversity loss because of land conversion. The latter concept – global market failure – relates to the fact that biodiversity conservation yields external benefits to people outside the boundaries of the nation faced with the development/conservation choice.

All these forms of failure can co-exist. Moreover, they exist very often in a context of rapidly changing population as far as developing countries are concerned. But these forms of failure are not peculiar to developing countries. Rich countries also have local market failure and government failure as well. They may have less global failure because the biodiversity that has global value is often, but not always, in developing or transition economies. Figure 4.1 summarizes the situation.

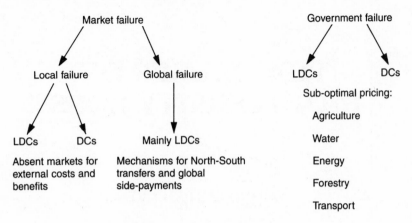

Figure 4.1 *Categories of economic failure*

Figure 4.2 introduces a diagrammatic exposition of the types of economic failure. The horizontal axis shows the amount of land converted to, say, agriculture. The vertical axis shows money. The downward sloping line MPB_i is the 'marginal private benefits' of land conversion, ie the extra revenue obtained by the farmer by converting the land from forest to agriculture. The line MC_i is the marginal cost to the farmer of making the conversion. The 'rational farmer' will equate MC_i and MPB_i in order to maximise profits.[1] Hence the amount of land conversion that actually takes place is L_P.

Now suppose the farmer is subsidized to convert the land. The effect can be shown as a lowering of MC_i to $MC_i - SUB$, where SUB refers to the subsidy. That is, private costs are lowered. This induces the landowner to expand the level of land conversion to L_{P+S}. The distance $L_P - L_{P+S}$ is a measure of *government failure* (GF).

What should the level of land conversion be ? To find this we

---

1 To see this, profits, π,equal $PB(L) - C(L)$, ie the private revenues from conversion less the costs of conversion. Maximizing profits and differentiating gives

$$d\pi/dL = dPB/dL - dC/dL = 0$$

or $$dPB/dL = dC/dL$$

But the left hand expression is marginal private benefits (MPB_i) and the right hand expression is marginal cost (MC_i).

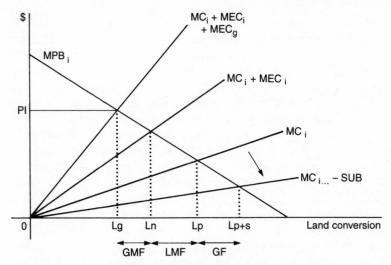

Figure 4.2 *Measuring economic failure*

need to estimate the value of the two externality components: the local and global externality. This involves *valuation*. If we know the value of the damage done to the nation from such land conversion – eg lost indirect and direct use values – then some estimate of the local external cost can be made. The diagram shows this as MEC_i, ie the marginal external cost imposed on the nation. If this externality is 'internalized', ie if the farmer is made to account for it in some way (eg by taxation or by bearing higher costs because the land is zoned for conservation) then the relevant 'optimum' moves to L_n. Note that L_n is less than L_P, so that internalizing the externality involves less land conversion and hence more biodiversity conservation. The distance $L_n - L_P$ is a measure of the *local market failure* (LMF).

The same procedure can be used to account for the global externality, the value of the losses borne by people outside the nation that owns the forest. The distance $L_G - L_N$ is a measure of *global market failure* or *global appropriation failure* (GMF).

The analysis also provides us with a rule for the 'proper pricing' of land. It is given by:

$$P_L = MC_i + MEC_i + MEC_g$$

and this is shown on the diagram. In other words, if land could be priced at the cost of its conversion *plus* the external costs of conversion, then the amount of conversion would be economically 'optimal'. Note that this optimal amount of land conversion is not zero – some deforestation still takes place. This result of the economic analysis is often regarded by environmentalists as unsatisfactory. Indeed, if one adopts the 'moral' standpoint discussed at the end of Chapter 3 it will appear to be 'immoral' to allow *any* deforestation to take place. This illustrates a further contrast between the economic and the moral standpoint: the latter tends to focus on the costs of deforestation *only*. It ignores the benefits of deforestation, ie the gains to be obtained by the farmer in question. The economic approach quite explicitly compares these benefits with the costs.

How does population growth and economic growth fit into the picture in Figure 4.2 ? It can be illustrated by shifting the MPB curve to the right over time. If the costs of further land conversion do not change (which they might as the 'frontier' gets further and further from established urban centres), then such shifts will make it more worthwhile to convert land. The reader can experiment with the diagram to see that all the 'optima' move to the right if the MPB curve shifts outwards.

Clearly, then, if there is to be a policy on biodiversity conservation it has to focus on the main fundamental causes of loss identified in this section:

- local market failure which will need to be addressed by local measures such as the zoning of land to forbid, say, forest burning;
- global market failure which will need to be addressed by 'creating' markets in global value and ensuring that compensation for forgoing the development option is paid to the landowner;
- intervention failure which will need to be addressed by showing the government that there are gains to be made by avoiding expensive policies of subsidization of forest clearance;
- limitation of population growth.

ILLUSTRATING ECONOMIC FAILURE: INTERVENTION FAILURE

Examples of intervention failure are, by now, well known (Pearce and Warford, 1993) and include the subsidies to forest conversion for livestock in Brazil up to the end of the 1980s; the subsidies to beef in Botswana, inflated by preferential tariffs in the European Community; hedgerow removal and over-intensive farming arising from above-equilibrium guaranteed prices under the European Common Agricultural Policy; the under-pricing of irrigation water whether in California or Pakistan, and so on. What government intervention does is to distort the competitive playing field. We are used to hearing businesspeople adopt this language, but, while they often see environmental regulations as the means of hampering their competitive efficiency, the truth is that the same argument shows powerfully why the conservation of biological diversity is an uphill struggle. Governments effectively subsidise the rate of return to land conversion, tilting the economic balance against conservation.

Table 4.1 assembles some information on the scale of the distortions that governments introduce. Such distortions are widespread. While some OECD countries tax their agricultural sectors, most subsidize agriculture. The extent of these subsidies is measured by the Producer Subsidy Equivalent (PSE)[2] which indicates the proportion of revenues farmers derive from various price support mechanisms. Table 4.1a indicates how for much of the '80s overall support has *increased* considerably. The aggregate figures disguise marked differences between farm products, with some arable crops benefiting from support in excess of 90 per cent. In the developing world, agricultural prices tend to be kept *below* their comparable border price for distributional reasons. On the other hand *input prices* for products such as pesticides and fertilizers are frequently subsidized, to the detriment of traditional integrated pest management systems. The effects of excessive use on mortality and related ecological problems have been well documented (Repetto, 1985).

---

2 A PSE equals:

$$Q.(P-PWnc) + DP - LV + OS$$

and a percentage PSE equals:

$$PSE/(Q.P + DP - LV)$$

where Q = volume of production; P = domestic producer price; PWnc = border price in national currency; DP = direct payments; LV = levies on production; OS = other support.

Table 4.1a OECD agricultural subsidies

	Producer subsidy equivalents		
	1981–84	1985–88	1989–92
Australia	11	12	12
Canada	30	47	45
EC	32	47	46
Japan	63	74	68
Sweden	38	55	57
United States	27	35	27
OECD	33	46	43

Source: OECD (1993)

Table 4.1b Agriculturarl input subsidies in developing countries

	Irrigation: Ratio of prices to capital + operating costs	Pesticides: Subsidy as a % of retail cost
Bangladesh	18*	
Indonesia	14	82
Rep of Korea	18	
Nepal	7	
Philippines	22	
Thailand	5	
China		19
Colombia		44
Ecuador		41
Egypt		83
Ghana		67
Senegal		89

* Operating costs only
Source: Pearce and Warford (1993)

Intervention failure is not confined to agriculture. Other notable sectors include commercial energy (Kosmo, 1989), where support may be costly both environmentally and in terms of diverted government revenues. The effects of regional incentives are sometimes less apparent but no less damaging. Historic use of investment, tax and credit incentives, as well as subsidized infrastructure, in the Brazilian Amazon have all raised the return to agriculture relative to forest conservation. Elsewhere, interventions which artificially inflate financial returns to timber production have the same effect. Most notable are the use of foreign investment tax breaks and low royalties or concession fees.

ILLUSTRATING ECONOMIC FAILURE: GLOBAL APPROPRIATION FAILURE

We can illustrate the phenomenon of 'missing markets' with two examples which are highly relevant to biodiversity: the 'non-use' or 'existence' value possessed by individuals in one country for wildlife and habitat in other countries, and the 'indirect use' carbon storage values of tropical forests. Global appropriation failure arises because these values are not easily captured or appropriated by the countries in possession of biological resources.

Non-use values

Economists use methods of measuring individual preferences, as revealed through individuals' 'willingness to pay' to conserve biodiversity. The methodologies include *contingent valuation* (CVM), which functions through sophisticated questionnaires which ask people their willingness to pay, and other techniques such as the *travel cost method*, the *hedonic property price* approach and the *production function* approach – see Chapter 5. The economic values that are captured in this way are likely to be a mix of potential use and non-use values. Use values relate to the valuation placed on the resource because the respondent makes use of it or might wish to make use of it in the future. Non-use values, or 'passive use values' as they are also called, relate to positive willingness to pay even if the respondent makes no use of the resource and has no intention of making use of it.

'Global valuations' of this kind are still few and far between. Table 4.2 assembles the results of CVMs in several countries. These report willingness to pay for species and habitat conservation in the respondents' own countries. These studies remain controversial, especially in light of the findings of the recent 'blue ribbon' panel on contingent valuation in the US (Arrow et al, 1993), although that same panel basically gave CVM a good bill of health provided rigorous rules of investigation are pursued. While

Table 4.2 *Preference valuations for endangered species and prized habitats*

Species		Preference valuations (US 1990 $ pa per person)
Norway:	brown bear, wolf and wolverine	15.0
USA:	bald eagle	12.4
	emerald shiner	4.5
	grizzly bear	18.5
	bighorn sheep	8.6
	whooping crane	1.2
	blue whale	9.3
	bottlenose dolphin	7.0
	California sea otter	8.1
	Northern elephant seal	8.1
	humpback whales[1]	40–48 (without information)
		49–64 (with information)
Habitat		
USA:	Grand Canyon (visibility)	27.0
	Colorado wilderness	9.3–21.2
Australia:	Nadgee Nature Reserve NSW	28.1
	Kakadu Conservation	40.0 (minor damage)
	Zone, NT[2]	93.0 (major damage)
UK:	nature reserves[3]	40.0 ('experts' only)
Norway:	conservation of rivers	59.0–107.0

Notes: (1) respondents divided into two groups, one of which was given video information; (2) two scenarios of mining development damage were given to respondents; (3) survey of informed 'expert' individuals only.
Source: Pearce (1993)

we cannot say that similar kinds of expressed values will arise for protection of biodiversity in other countries, even a benchmark figure of, say, $10 pa per person for the rich countries of Europe and North America would produce a fund of $4 billion pa. This is around four times the mooted size of the fund that will be available to the Global Environment facility in its operational phase as the financial mechanism under the two Rio Conventions and in the context of its continuing role in capturing global values from the international waters (see Chapter 8), and perhaps 10 times what the Fund will have available for helping with biodiversity conservation under the Rio Convention.

Carbon storage

All forests store carbon so that, if cleared for agriculture, there will be a release of carbon dioxide which will contribute to accelerating the greenhouse effect and hence global warming. In order to derive a value for the 'carbon credit' that should be ascribed to a tropical forest, we need to know (1) the net carbon released when forests are converted to other uses, and (2) the economic value of one tonne of carbon released to the atmosphere.

Carbon will be released at different rates according to the method of clearance and subsequent land use. With burning there will be an immediate release of CO_2 into the atmosphere, and some of the remaining carbon will be locked in ash and charcoal which is resistant to decay. The slash not converted by fire into CO_2 or charcoal and ash decays over time, releasing most of its carbon to the atmosphere within 10–20 years. Studies of tropical forests indicate that significant amounts of cleared vegetation become lumber, slash, charcoal and ash. The proportion differs for closed and open forests; the smaller stature and drier climate of open forests result in the combustion of higher proportion of the vegetation.

If tropical forested land is converted to pasture or permanent agriculture, then the amount of carbon stored in secondary vegetation is equivalent to the carbon content of the biomass of crops planted, or the grass grown on the pasture. If a secondary forest is allowed to grow, then carbon will accumulate, and maximum biomass density is attained after a relatively short time.

Table 4.3 illustrates the net carbon storage effects of land use

Table 4.3 *Changes in carbon with land use conversion (tC/ha)*

	Original C	Shifting agriculture	Permanent agriculture	Pasture
Original C		79	63	63
Closed primary	283	−204	−220	−220
Closed secondary	194	−106	−152	−122
Open forest	115	−36	−52	−52

Shifting agriculture represents carbon in biomass and soils in second year of shifting cultivation cycle.

Source: Brown and Pearce (1994)

conversion from tropical forests (closed primary, closed secondary, or open forests) to shifting cultivation, permanent agriculture, or pasture. The negative figures represent emissions of carbon; for example, conversion from closed primary forest to shifting agriculture results in a net loss of 194 tC/ha. The greatest loss of carbon involves change of land use from primary closed forest to permanent agriculture. These figures represent the once and for all change that will occur in carbon storage as a result of the various land use conversions.

The data suggest that, allowing for the carbon fixed by subsequent land uses, carbon released from deforestation of secondary and primary tropical forest is of the order of 100–200 tonnes of carbon per hectare.[3]

The carbon released from burning tropical forests contributes to global warming, and we now have several estimates of the minimum economic damage done by global warming, leaving aside catastrophic events. Recent work by Fankhauser (1994) suggests a 'central' value of $20 of damage for every tonne of carbon released. Applying this figure to the data in Table 4.3, we can conclude that converting an open forest to agriculture or pasture would result in global warming damage of, say, $600–1000 per hectare; conversion of closed secondary forest would cause damage of $2000–3000 per hectare; and conversion of primary forest to agriculture would give rise to damage of about $4000–4400 per hectare. Note that these estimates allow for carbon fixation in the subsequent land use.

How do these estimates relate to the development benefits of land use conversion? We can illustrate with respect to the Amazon region of Brazil. Schneider (1992) reports upper bound values of $300 per hectare for land in Rondonia. The figures suggest carbon credit values two to fifteen times the price of land in Rondonia. These 'carbon credits' also compare favourably with the value of forest land for timber in, say, Indonesia, where estimates are of the order of $2000–2500 per hectare. All this suggests scope for a global bargain. The land is worth $300 per hectare to the forest colonist but several times this to the world at large. If the North can

---

3 A refinement to these figures would estimate the present value of the carbon releases by discounting future carbon releases. That is, all the carbon is not released in the initial burning. There may be subsequent burnings, and there may be some slower release of carbon over time.

transfer a sum of money greater than $300 but less than the damage cost from global warming, there are mutual gains to be obtained.

Note that if the transfers did take place at, say, $500 per hectare, then the cost per tonne of carbon reduced is of the order of $5 tC ($500/100 tC/ha). These unit costs compare favourably with those achieved by carbon emission reduction policies through fossil fuel conversion. Avoiding deforestation becomes a legitimate and potentially important means of reducing global warming rates.

THE DISTRIBUTION OF CONSERVATION COSTS AND BENEFITS

Figure 4.2 demonstrated the economic rationality of land conversion when accounting for the global and national as well as private costs. Valuation of these externalities turns out to be a prerequisite for moving towards a 'globally efficient' rate of conversion. In the case of forest conversion for example, values for carbon storage are more readily quantified than those of biodiversity. Uncertainty in benefit and cost accounting suggests that there cannot be a completely certain view of the optimal conversion level, nor what the optimal policy to reach it will look like. Economic valuation *can*, however, help move in the direction of an economically efficient or 'first best' outcome. While this might make conservation policy seem like a hit and miss affair, greater precision will emerge with improved scientific understanding of ecological processes and a political appreciation of a latent global WTP for conservation.

Translating the economic rationality into effective national and local incentives is an equally challenging policy issue. As noted elsewhere, conservation in many countries is characterized by a spatial mismatch between costs and benefits (Wells, 1992a). In other words, economic benefits from conserved areas tend to be limited on a local scale, increase somewhat at a national level and, as is slowly becoming clear, can be substantial on a global scale. On the other hand, costs, in terms of forgone development benefits, tend to be locally significant and nationally and globally moderate. Appraising conservation policies in a cost-benefit framework, it is tempting to abstract from these distributional issues, providing an intervention increases aggregate welfare and gainers could *potentially* compensate the losers. The capacity for potential compensation is a common assumption in welfare economics, and economists term such welfare-generating changes 'net welfare gains'. In the context of global conservation, the emphasis on potential rather than *actual* compensation is clearly misplaced. As incomes rise and pristine environments suffer greater degradation, global demand for conservation for ecotourism, recreation and other non-use benefits is likely to increase. Since many highly prized environments are in countries where conservation has high opportunity costs, meeting this global demand without compensation will accentuate the benefit mismatch. The problem is clear. A wider population of global beneficiaries from conservation habitually demonstrates a willingness to pay for conservation by visiting wildlife sites, subscribing to conservation groups or simply for the option of visiting or using indigenous resources. This demand restricts revenue opportunities for local populations who in effect subsidize the provision of a global public good.[4] The remedy would therefore seem straightforward. Either sufficient appropriable local benefits derive from, say, improved participation in conservation provision, or a system of international compensation is formulated. In an ideal world the latter would occur through a market for conservation goods. Such *global environmental markets* (GEMs), although historically 'missing', are beginning to emerge albeit on a modest scale (Pearce, 1994 and Chapter 8). Public (official) ventures of this nature include disbursements under the Global Environment Facility, officially sanctioned debt-swaps and debt rescheduling. Private initiatives generally relate directly to existing legislation which price externalities and provide scope for mutually beneficial trades. Carbon off-set agreements are probably the clearest example (Faeth et al, 1994).

In the context of biodiversity conservation, most GEM transactions are at a national level, the exception being a number of private prospecting contracts for plant genetic materials (Gamez et al, 1993). What incentives these agreements provide at a household level is far from certain. Indeed, international transactions may be to limited effect if they cannot be applied and enforced where it matters most. Drawing on developed country experience, conservation easements, compensated set-aside and tradeable

---

4 In economics, the term *public good* refers to a good or service where consumption is 'non-rival' and 'non-exclusive'. This non-excludability characterizes benefits such as existence and option values.

development rights have all been suggested as potential mechanisms for effecting workable agreements (Katzman and Cale, 1990; Cervigni, 1993a; Panayotou, 1994). The characteristics of these trades include appropriable mutual gains to participating landowners and sponsoring public or private organizations, and incentive compatibility. In other words, agreements must be structured so as to maximize the incentive to comply, while minimizing both the gains from cheating and policing costs at each level of administration and operation. While experience with such instruments is limited, not least by complex national and international legal implications, they are a promising attempt at bridging the gap (establishing channels) between benefit provision, global transfers and local appropriation.

5

METHODOLOGIES FOR ECONOMIC VALUATION

INTRODUCTION: VALUATION IN HIGH AND LOW INCOME CONTEXTS

Chapters 3 and 4 described the philosophy underlying the procedure for putting money values on preferences for environmental change. This chapter investigates the *methodologies* for eliciting economic values. A potentially important issue arises in that much of the world's threatened biological diversity is in the *developing world*, whereas the theory and practice of economic valuation has been developed and applied mainly in the *developed world*. Accordingly, it is important to assess whether rich country methodologies can be applied in poor country contexts. Prima facie, it could be argued that a number of the methodologies will not be applicable due to the absence of even moderately freely functioning markets for inputs (eg labour, capital, raw materials) and outputs (eg agricultural produce) in developing countries. In practice, there is a fairly extensive literature on the valuation of environmental change in developing countries and, by and large, the problems of application, while significant, are not insuperable.

It has been shown that procedures which require individuals to state their 'willingness to pay' in hypothetical contexts for goods and services (contingent valuation), work well in most developing country contexts (Whittington et al, 1991; Boadu, 1992). As in any developed country, the respondent faces a budget constraint (income or wealth) and, provided he or she is familiar with the good being offered, responses in developing country contexts appear to be as reliable as in other contexts. Other techniques observe actual behaviour and infer valuations based on that behaviour. For example, if water users have three options facing them – water being brought to the door, water purchased from a local 'kiosk', and getting water from a fairly distant well – it is possible to value the time spent collecting the well water by looking at the differences in prices in the three options ('discrete choice' approach). Additionally, approaches which link some change in an environmental variable to a change in a marketed output provide us with a potentially large set of estimates. This is, for example, how most studies on the economic costs of soil erosion have been carried out.

Extending these procedures to the valuation of biological diversity is complex. Indeed, the valuation of preferences for biodiversity is perhaps the most challenging issue in the context of economic valuation. But there are many use values, such as ecotourism, in which various valuation procedures (such as the travel cost method) might be used. Similarly, surveys measuring the forgone local use benefits from reserve designation or tourists' willingness to pay for park maintenance provide some guidance for conservation policy (Mercer et al, 1993; Moran, 1994). The focus of these studies is on the conservation of biological resources, but there may often be incidental diversity benefits if subjects are considered to be keystones or whole system pivots.

To date, procedures whereby individuals are asked their willingness to pay to conserve biodiversity *per se* have not been used in the developing country context. In developed countries, direct questioning on biodiversity preferences is largely limited to the preservation of well-known or 'charismatic' species and ecosystems. Recent attempts to elicit preferences for less familiar biodiversity have encountered response difficulties when subject goods are difficult to explain or unknown to respondents, or where respondents lack experience of making similar transactions (Stevens et al, 1991; Hanley and Spash, 1993). The issue of whether value statements are the result of an information constraint or a more fundamental refusal to make implicit trade-offs, is yet to be resolved.

Valuations of the *sustainable uses* of habitat have been carried out, eg for medicinal plants and non-timber forest products. Hence there is considerable scope for at least securing minimum values for biological diversity through the use of approaches focused on market values.

A CLASSIFICATION OF VALUATION PROCEDURES

There are basically two broad approaches to valuation, each comprising a number of techniques:

1 direct approaches; and
2 indirect approaches.

The direct approach looks at techniques which attempt to elicit preferences directly by the use of survey and experimental techniques, such as the contingent valuation and contingent ranking methods. People are asked directly to state or reveal their strength of preference for a proposed change. In contrast, indirect approaches are those techniques which seek to elicit preferences from actual, observed market based information. Preferences for the environmental good are revealed indirectly when an individual purchases a marketed good to which the environmental good is related in some way.

THE DIRECT VALUATION APPROACH

In the direct approach, an attempt is made to elicit preferences by either experiments or questionnaires.

Experiments
If an analyst wanted to know how much people value a potential new recreation site, the recreation site could be created and an entrance fee charged. The analyst then observes how many people actually use the site, in effect exchanging money for the recreation and aesthetic experience of visiting the site. Alternatively, if the analyst wanted to know how much people would be willing to pay to live in a city with improved water quality, water quality standards and property taxes would be raised in some cities and not in others. The analyst could then see how many people found it worthwhile to move to cities with improved water quality and higher taxes. In practice, large scale experiments of this type are very difficult to design and implement, although small scale experiments have been carried out successfully.

Questionnaires (surveys)
There are two types of questioning that can be undertaken:

1 *Eliciting Rankings* – this is similar to contingent valuation (see below) except that the questioner is content to obtain a ranking of preferences which can later be 'anchored' by the analyst in a real price of something observed in the market. This is known as the *Contingent Ranking Method* (CRM).

2 *Eliciting Values* – people are asked directly to state or reveal 'what they are willing to pay (WTP) for some change in provision of a good or service or to prevent a change' and/or 'what they are willing to accept (WTA) to forgo a change or tolerate the change'. A contingent market encompasses the good itself, the institutional context in which it would be provided, and the way it would be financed. The situation the respondent is asked to value is hypothetical and respondents are assumed to behave in an identical way to that in a real market. Structured questions and various forms of 'bidding game' can be devised, involving 'yes/no' answers to questions regarding maximum willingness to pay. Econometric techniques are then used on the survey results to find the mean bid values of willingness to pay. This is known as the *Contingent Valuation Method* (CVM), and measures precisely what the analyst wants to know – the individual's strength of preferences for the proposed change – and can be used not only for non-marketed goods and services, but for market goods as well. If people were able to understand clearly the change in environmental quality being offered, and answered truthfully, this direct approach would be ideal. However the central problem with the approach is whether the intentions people indicate *ex-ante* (before the change) will accurately describe their behaviour *ex-post* (after the change) when they face no penalty or cost associated with a discrepancy between the two. This is known as 'strategic bias' and occurs if there is a 'free rider' problem.

The contingent valuation method

Interest in CVM has increased over the last decade or so because, firstly, it will be the only means available for valuing non-use values – the values obtained from indirect techniques are not aimed at capturing non-use values. Secondly, estimates obtained from well designed, properly executed surveys appear to be as good as estimates obtained from other methods. Thirdly, the design, analysis and interpretation of surveys have improved greatly as scientific sampling theory, benefit estimation theory, computerized data management and public opinion polling have improved.

There are three basic parts to most CV survey instruments:

1   A hypothetical description (scenario) of the terms under which the good or service is to be offered is presented to the respondent. This will include information on when the service will be available, how the respondent will be expected to pay for it, how much others will be expected to pay, what institutions will be responsible for delivery of the service, the quality and reliability of the service.

2   The respondent is asked questions to determine how much he would value a good or service if confronted with the opportunity to obtain it under the specified terms and conditions. These questions take the form of asking how much an individual is WTP or WTA for some change in provision. Depending on the preferred elicitation format, econometric models are then used to infer a WTP for the change. An aggregate welfare measure can be calculated by multiplying a favoured measure of response central tendency (mean or median) over a relevant population of users.

3   Response validity is tested by relating WTP responses to respondent socioeconomic and demographic characteristics. Confirmation of *a priori* expectations of the relationship between WTP income, age and other variables is a good indication of meaningful responses.

CVM: elicitation, bias and acceptability

Respondents can indicate their choice or preference in a number of ways. One is to answer questions relating to whether or not they would want to purchase the service if it cost a specified amount. These are known as discrete or *dichotomous* choice questions. Another possibility is to ask respondents direct questions about the most they would be willing to pay for the good or service – known as continuous or open-ended questions. These two types can be combined in a CV questionnaire to create different ways of eliciting the valuation information, eg a bidding game. In addition, respondents may be shown a list of possible answers in the form of a 'payment' card, and asked to indicate their choice, although this requires a careful determination of the range of possible answers.

The appropriate choice for a specific problem is a matter of judgement on the part of the analyst. Many recent studies have opted for the dichotomous choice format for its bias-reducing properties. In other words a 'take it or leave it' question approximates a market transaction familiar to most respondents and minimizes the incentive to give a strategic response (see below). Choice of format also matters because the determination of mean or median WTP measures from yes-no data requires a higher degree of statistical competence. In essence, the required analysis uses qualitative choice models to calculate an expected mean WTP value (see Loomis, 1988). There is no one correct procedure for this analysis, and several of the assumptions routinely employed are the subject of current debate among practitioners (Hanemann, 1984, 1989; Johansson et al, 1989).

An assessment of the technical acceptability of CVM involves looking at various methodological issues, which we divide into issues of reliability, bias and validity.

Reliability: This looks at the degree to which the variance of WTP responses are attributable to random error. The greater is the degree of non-randomness, the less the reliability of the study, such that mean WTP answers are of little value. The variance arises as a consequence of true random error (essential to the statistical process); sampling procedure (variance is minimized by ensuring a statistically significant sample size); the questionnaire/interview itself (it is important for reliability to ensure that the CVM scenario is as realistic and familiar to the respondent as possible). In order to assess reliability, a number of practitioners have advocated the use of replicability tests, ie repeating an experiment using different samples to see if there is correlation between the variables collected. Though few such tests have been carried out in practice due to their expense, Heberlein (1986); Loehman and De (1982) and Loomis (1989, 1990) have undertaken such testing and found significant correlation between WTP in the test and retest.

Bias: A number of different types of bias can be identified:

1 *Strategic bias* – the problem of strategic bias has long worried economists. The behaviour necessary for this kind of bias depends on the respondent's perceived payment obligation and his expectation about the provision of a good. Where indivi-

duals actually have to pay their reported WTP values then there is the temptation to understate their true preferences in the hope of a free ride. Or, if the price to be charged for the good is not tied to an individual's WTP response, but the provision of the good is, then over-reporting of WTP may occur in order to ensure provision. Empirical investigations of strategic bias are well documented. One approach to testing for strategic bias argues that if true WTP bids are theoretically normally distributed, strategic behaviour would bias this distribution towards zero (Brookshire et al, 1976). However this test has been criticized on the grounds that bimodal distributions can be posited on the income characteristics of the respondent population. Minimization of occurrence of strategic behaviour can be achieved by framing the CVM questions in an incentive compatible way such that this type of behaviour is not induced. One particular approach is to ask respondents to make bids for a good under three scenarios – only the highest bidders get the good; everyone gets the good if WTP is above a certain level; everyone with a positive WTP gets the good. The first scenario is assumed to give true WTP, the second has a weak free-riding incentive and the third a strong one. Empirical evidence suggests that the two latter scenarios do indeed produce WTP values below their true level. Such findings tend to come from open-ended format questions rather than discrete response approaches, where free-riding behaviour is likely to be minimized. Some authors suggest implementation of a property rights approach, in which respondents receive provision of a good relative to their given WTP in order to remove free riding. This is not applicable for most environmental public goods for which non-use and altruistic values act as a disincentive to free ride anyway. Overall, strategic bias problems have not been found to be a significant problem in practice.

2 *Hypothetical bias* – the hypothetical nature of the market in CV studies can render respondents' answers meaningless if their declared intentions cannot be taken as accurate guides of their actual behaviour. Some writers have looked at hypothetical bias in terms of increased bid variance and low model reliability, whereas others view the use of hypothetical markets as having other distinct problems. Research into hypothetical markets and their predictive ability has looked at the attitude-behaviour

relationship, and experiments examining substitution of real for hypothetical markets.

The Fishbein-Azjen attitude behaviour model (1975) looks at the links between stated attitudes and actual behaviour. In order to minimize hypothetical bias, this model argues that the specified attitude (WTP scenario) must closely correspond to the specified behaviour (the precise good measured). Secondly, predictive power will be greater, the fewer the influencing relationships between a component in the model and behaviour. Thirdly, where a respondent is dealing with familiar behavioural situations, then attitude will be a better predictor of behaviour.

A survey of experimental tests reveals that by using a WTP format instead of a WTA format, hypothetical bias, which may be a significant problem in WTA studies, can be reduced to an insignificant level. The tests usually compare the hypothetical bids with bids obtained in simulated markets where real money transactions have taken place. Results from such studies suggest that the divergence between actual and hypothetical WTP is much less than that for WTA, the reason being that respondents are more familiar with payment rather than compensation scenarios (Hanley, 1990).

3 *The embedding problem* – there is evidence to suggest that people have problems understanding certain kinds of questions that depend on insights into their own feelings or their memory of events or feelings. This kind of problem will be very apparent in environmental issues because they evoke deeply held moral, philosophical and religious beliefs. One particular problem in this vein much looked at, is that respondents may interpret the hypothetical offers of a specific good or service to be indicative of an offer for a broader set of similar goods and services. This is known as the embedding problem since the value of the good being sought is embedded in the value of the more encompassing set of goods or services reported by the respondent. This problem is indicative of an even broader problem with obtaining accurate answers. For a single individual the total amount they are WTP for improved environmental goods and services may be determined by the composition or components of the total set of environmental projects and policies to be funded. However this information is unlikely to be obtained

from the aggregation of values based on a set of CV studies designed to measure individuals' preferences for narrowly defined environmental goods. Kahneman and Knetsch (1992) provide recent empirical evidence of embedding in a study looking at WTP for maintaining the quality of fishing lakes. Individuals were instead thought to purchase moral satisfaction in their WTP responses. This study was criticized on the grounds of having a poor instrument design – using telephone surveys, poor information – a single sentence to describe the good, and problems with the actual question framing rather than the underlying theory, which resulted in embedding. Problems remain with embedding. Willis and Garrod (1991) set the problem in the context of the theory of two-stage budgeting, where total income is firstly allocated to broad expenditure categories and then, secondly, subdivided within categories among specific items. Several mental accounts are thus set up, each referring to a category. Thus in responding to questionnaires, individuals may not consider the limits to, and other demands upon, their relevant mental account. This omission lies at the heart of the problem and is addressed by asking respondents to calculate total yearly budget for all environmental issues. Willis and Garrod (1991) test this for the Yorkshire Dales National Park and find no significant evidence of the problem. This result is supported by other similar studies. A variant of the problem is where WTP for a category group of goods is less than the sum of WTP responses regarding the specific good contents of that category, ie where WTP is asked in the context of other goods then this amount may tend to be less than if asked in isolation of other goods. Empirical evidence is mixed. Some studies have extended this contextual problem and found an ordering effect such that the higher a good is up a list of goods to be valued, the higher the WTP response.

4 *Information bias* – the quality of information given in a hypo-thetical market scenario almost certainly affects the responses received. Empirical evidence suggests only a weak information bias with some studies finding a threshold effect for information build up, below which no bias is detectable but above which a positive and weak effect is found. Other studies have found no significant information bias, though bid variance was found to fall as information increased. A number of writers have argued

that information will always affect WTP but that this result applies to all goods, be they public or private. In the context of unknown or lesser order species, the issue of information provision as the basis of a valuation response is clearly vital. If CV use is to be extended beyond celebrated species and ecosystems, the effects of information provision must be addressed. Few experimental studies have investigated the extent of an information threshold in the context of biodiversity values. One current debate among practitioners is, however, jammed on an analogous issue of an information constraint on the validity of existence value statements (NOAA, 1994). More specifically, should uninformed respondents be informed, and how does this process affect their eventual responses to CV questions? If there is no information provision, should the responses of uninformed respondents count, and what does this imply for the range of subjects suitable for CV studies?

5 *Aggregation bias* – there may be problems in aggregating individual valuation responses. Analysts will often wish to summarize respondents' answers to valuation questions in terms of the mean willingness to pay for the good or service, or develop an aggregate benefit estimate for a community or region. Two types of problems here are sampling errors and insufficient sample size. Sampling errors include a non-random sample being selected and used. This may result from non-responses to the questions. Non-responses are more likely to occur for certain types of individuals who are not randomly distributed in the population. If the size of the sample is small, there is a risk that the characteristics of the sample will not be representative of the general population, thus resulting in findings which suffer wide confidence intervals. Furthermore, non-normal WTP distributions can cause the sample mean to be biased by the major tail of the distribution, necessitating the use of truncated means as an aggregate measure of welfare.

   Often, on-site surveys will ignore the non-use values held by non-visitors such that additional random sample off-site surveys will be needed to estimate non-use values. Empirical studies have found total non-use value is significant and can even exceed total use value.

6 *Interviewer and respondent bias* – the way interviewers conduct themselves and interviews can influence responses. Bias can be

minimized by using mail or telephone surveys though this can mean less information is forthcoming and give rise to hypothetical bias. Mail surveys also give low response rates. Another variant of this problem is compliance bias, whereby the respondent tries to guess the 'correct' answer or not give the questions proper considerations. To minimize this problem professional interviewers should be used, and they should follow the wording of the questionnaire *exactly*, with the respondents being offered a choice of prepared responses.

7 *Payment vehicle bias* – a number of studies have found that WTP varies depending on whether an income tax increase or an entrance fee is used as a payment vehicle (method of payment for the good). To minimize this bias, controversial payment vehicles should be avoided and a method used which is most likely to be used in real life to elicit payment for the good in question.

8 *Starting point, anchoring and discrete bid level bias* – The suggestion of an initial starting point in a bidding game can significantly influence the final bid, eg choosing a low (high) starting point leads to a low (high) mean WTP. The use of starting points can reduce the amount of non-responses and the variance in open-ended type questionnaires, though it also may result in respondents not giving their answer serious thought and taking a cognitive short cut in arriving at their decision. One solution to this problem is the use of what is called a 'payment card' whereby the respondent selects a bid from a range shown on the card. However this can result in an 'anchoring' of bids within the range of bids asked. Optimal bids should be set such that the lowest bid results in all respondents accepting it, and the highest bid results in all respondents rejecting it. Within this range, bid levels should reflect the distribution of bids so that, optimally, each bid interval reflects the same proportion of the population. A recent study by Bateman et al (1992), used a large sample open-ended format WTP question in order to estimate the distribution and range of WTP bids. A bid function was then estimated such that a probability of discrete bid acceptance curve could be mapped out. Eight WTP bid levels were subsequently chosen for a dichotomous choice experiment. The results were compared with an open-ended experiment and it was found that a dichotomous choice respondent

was more likely to assent to the question 'are you WTP £x?' than an open-ended respondent is likely to state a WTP of £x or above. Several factors may have influenced this result. Open-ended format studies are subject to free rider problems whereas dichotomous choice is not; dichotomous choice formats may be subject to interviewer bias and are more likely to exhibit anchoring bias, thereby biasing upwards the mean WTP. To conclude, open-ended approaches are likely to provide a lower bound WTP estimate below which true WTP is unlikely to lie, while dichotomous choice approaches provide an upper bound WTP estimate above which true WTP is unlikely to lie.

Validity: There are three categories of validity testing used in CVM studies:

1 *Content validity* – this looks at whether the WTP measure estimated in a CV study accurately corresponds to the object being looked at (the construct). Such testing cannot be formalized, resulting in analysts having to decide in a subjective manner whether a CVM has asked the correct questions appropriately, and if the WTP measure is in fact what respondents would actually pay for a public good if a market existed. Five 'Reference Operating Conditions' have been proposed by Cummings et al (1986) for enhancing the validity of CV studies. It is thought that due to improvements in survey questionnaire design, content validity is not as great a problem as first thought.

2 *Criterion Validity* – here the CVM estimates are compared with the 'true' value (the criterion) of the good in question. This is not feasible for many environmental goods (and is why CVM is carried out in the first place). However experiments comparing hypothetical WTP sums from CVM with 'true' WTP, as determined by simulated markets using real money payments, have been carried out as mentioned in the earlier section on hypothetical bias. These find that in general, WTP format CVM studies give valid estimates of true WTP, though this is not the case for WTA.

3 *Construct validity* (including convergent and theoretical validity) – theoretical validity tests whether the CVM measure conforms to theoretical expectations, and convergent validity tests whe-

ther the CVM measure is closely correlated with measures of the good found using other valuation techniques.

Theoretical validity tests have centred on examining bid curve functions to see if they conform to theoretical expectations, eg whether elasticities are correctly signed and feasibly sized; tests on the significance of explanatory variables (by looking at simple 't' statistic tests, and the explanatory power of bid functions).

Convergent validity compares CVM measures with revealed preference techniques such as travel cost and hedonic pricing (see later). However the methods compared are usually measuring different theoretical constructs, eg, CVM measures use and non-use values whereas travel cost only measures use values. Furthermore, CVM provides *ex-ante* measures of WTP whilst hedonic pricing and travel cost estimates are from ex-post contexts. As such, the usefulness of convergent validity testing is not as great as at first thought.

Analysis of WTP responses

There are three ways in which CVM information is typically analysed:

1 Analysts examine the frequency distribution of the responses to the valuation questions.
2 Cross tabulations between WTP and socioeconomic variables, etc, are looked at.
3 Multivariate statistical techniques are used to estimate a valuation function that relates the respondent's answer to the socioeconomic characteristics of the respondent.

These analyses are used to see if respondents' answers are consistent with theory and to establish statistical relationships that can be used in the aggregation of sample responses to the overall population under study. Before the analyses can be undertaken, the data must be 'cleaned' by removing 'protest responses' of individuals who reject the hypothetical scenario and refuse to give meaningful answers. This can be done by setting an upper limit on how much a respondent's bid could be above the mean bid of the sample, or by seeing if respondents bidding very high or low have the socioeconomic characteristics that one would expect to be associated with such a response. Obviously such judgements are subjective and require careful consideration of field conditions, questionnaire, and analysis of the data.

Analysis of frequency distributions of WTP responses: Answers to open-ended valuation questions yield a set of point estimates of WTP. Statistics such as the mean, median and frequency distributions can be found for data sets of point estimates of WTP. Data such as mean estimates of WTP can provide estimates of total value of the good or service, alternatively the frequency distribution can be used to estimate the percentage of the population that would choose to purchase the good if it were offered at a specific price. Answers for dichotomous choice questions can be summarized in a way that provides similar information to the frequency distribution of point estimates described above. The percentage of respondents that agreed to pay each specified price can be found and then the relationship between these percentages and the price of the good can be graphed.

Cross tabulations of WTP responses with socioeconomic characteristics of the respondent and attitudes towards the environment: When point estimates of WTP are available for respondents, the analyst can calculate the mean WTP bid for different groups of respondents, so as to address the question of who is willing to pay the most for the good and why. If these cross tabulations of WTP bids and socioeconomic or attitudinal information reveal the effects one would expect from demand theory then the analyst has greater confidence in the quality of the data and greater insight into the factors that determine an individual's WTP. Cross tabulations for dichotomous choice questions are also possible but require large sample sizes since there may otherwise not be enough independent observations or degrees of freedom to carry out tests of differences between groups that have much statistical power.

Multivariate analyses of the determinants of WTP responses: Here the approach is to estimate a valuation function that relates the hypothesized determinants with the WTP responses. The determinants typically used include socioeconomic and demographic characteristics of the household and prices and availability of substitute goods and services. Open-ended questions will give a continuous measure of WTP for the good or service such that Ordinary Least Squares (OLS) models can be used to explain the variations in the dependent variable. OLS requires, of course, that the determinants of the WTP responses be exogenous in order for the parameter estimates to be unbiased and consistent. It is thought that if R^2 values for valuation functions fall below 0.15 then the credibility of the values should be called into question. For dichotomous choice questions the responses are discrete and so OLS is unsuitable for estimation of the valuation function. Instead a variety of discrete choice models are available to explain the probability that a respondent will give a *yes* response to the valuation question. Again, the same kind of independent variables as above are used to explain the respondents' answers. For computational ease, most studies use logit or probit models. Such discrete choice models can be used to derive estimates of the economic value of the good and also of the relationship between the percentage of respondents agreeing to pay and the price offered whilst controlling for socioeconomic characteristics of the respondents and other factors.

Conclusion on CVM

It is important to get accurate, reliable answers to CV questions. In a report to the US National Oceanic and Atmospheric Administration (NOAA) committee, Arrow et al (1993) have offered a set of guidelines that they believe CV researchers should follow in order to ensure that CV studies provide accurate, reliable information (see below). The best prospects for use of CVM are in attempting to find WTP for an environmental gain, and when familiar goods are being looked at such as local recreational amenities. WTP and WTA for environmental losses are more problematic. Despite the pedigree of the Nobel laureate panel, the guidelines are in no sense a last word in the CV debate. Persisting areas of disagreement range from reliability of small sample sizes to the issue of previous information. Similarly, few of the issues concerning the psychological and cognitive processes of response formulation have been definitively resolved (Willis, 1993; Schkade and Payne, 1994). Despite these reservations, CV remains a promising option for biodiversity valuation. As already noted, the technique is the only way to elicit non-use values directly. Secondly, the potential for information provision and exchange during the survey process or during respondent focus group exercises, or using verbal protocols ('think aloud analysis'), offers scope to experiment with respondent knowledge and understanding of biodiversity. Recent improvements on the CV design process, employing *stated preference methods* (SPM) offer similar promise (Adamowicz, 1994; Louviere, 1994). Developed in the marketing and transport fields, SPM elicit consumer responses to a broader range of subject resource attributes than normally employed in a CV survey. Lastly, even if specific CV surveys are deemed unreliable for use in cost-benefit appraisal or for legal purposes, they can at least be treated as a surrogate referendum for determining conservation priorities based on public preferences (Blamey and Common, 1993).

GUIDELINES FOR CONDUCTING CONTINGENT VALUATION STUDIES

(Adapted from the report of the National Oceanic and Atmospheric Administration Panel on the Contingent Valuation Method, Arrow et al, 1993)

GENERAL GUIDELINES

1 *Sample type and size* – probability sampling is essential. The choice of sample specific design and size is a difficult, technical question that requires the guidance of a professional sampling statistician.
2 *Minimize non-responses* – high non-response rates would make CV survey results unreliable.
3 *Personal interview* – it is unlikely that reliable estimates of values can be elicited with mail surveys. Face-to-face interviews are usually preferable, although telephone interviews have some advantages in terms of cost and centralized supervision.
4 *Pretesting for interviewer effects* – an important respect in which CV surveys differ from actual referendum is the presence of an interviewer (except in the case of mail surveys). It is possible that interviewers contribute to 'social desirability' bias, since preserving the environment is widely viewed as something positive. In order to test this possibility, major CV studies should incorporate experiments that assess interviewer effects.
5 *Reporting* – every report of a CV study should make clear the definition of the population sampled, the sampling frame used, the sample size, the overall sample non-response rate and its components (eg, refusals),

and item non-response on all important questions. The report should also reproduce the exact wording and sequence of the questionnaire and of other communications to respondents (eg, advance letters). All data from the study should be archived and made available to interested parties.

6   *Careful pretesting of a CV questionnaire* – respondents in a CV survey are ordinarily presented with a good deal of new and often technical information, well beyond what is typical in most surveys. This requires very careful pilot work and pretesting, plus evidence from the final survey that respondents understood and accepted the description of the good or service offered and the questioning reasonably well.

GUIDELINES FOR VALUE ELICITATION SURVEYS

7   *Conservative design* – when aspects of the survey design and the analysis of the responses are ambiguous, the option that tends to underestimate willingness to pay is generally preferred. A conservative design increases the reliability of the estimate by eliminating extreme responses that can enlarge estimated values wildly and implausibly.

8   *Elicitation format* – the willingness-to-pay format should be used instead of compensation required because the former is the conservative choice.

9   *Referendum format* – the valuation question generally should be posed as a vote on a referendum.

10 *Accurate description of the programme or policy* – adequate information must be provided to respondents about the environmental programme that is offered.

11 *Pretesting of photographs* – the effects of photographs on subjects must be carefully explored.

12 *Reminder of substitute commodities* – respondents must be reminded of substitute commodities. This reminder should be introduced forcefully and directly prior to the main valuation to assure that the respondents have the alternatives clearly in mind.

13 *Temporal averaging* – time dependent measurement noise should be reduced by averaging across independently drawn samples taken at different points in time. A clear and substantial time trend in the responses would cast doubt on the 'reliability' of the value information obtained from a CV survey.

14 *'No-answer' option* – a 'no-answer' option should be explicitly allowed in the addition to the 'yes' and 'no' vote options on the main valuation (referendum) question. Respondents who choose the 'no-answer' option should be asked to explain their choice.

15   *Yes/no follow-ups* – yes and no responses should be followed up by the open-ended question: 'Why did you vote yes/no?'

16   *Cross-tabulations* – the survey should include a variety of other questions that help interpret the responses to the primary valuation question. The final report should include summaries of willingness to pay broken down by these categories (eg, income, education, attitudes toward the environment).

17   *Checks on understanding and acceptance* – the survey instrument should not be so complex that it poses tasks that are beyond the ability or interest level of many participants.

THE INDIRECT VALUATION APPROACH

Indirect approaches are those techniques which seek to elicit preferences from actual, observed market based information. Preferences for the environmental good are revealed indirectly, when an individual purchases a marketed good which the environmental good is related to in some way. The techniques included here are as follows:

- hedonic price and wage techniques;
- the travel cost method;
- avertive behaviour; and
- dose-response and replacement cost techniques.

They are all indirect because they do not rely on people's direct answers to questions about how much they would be willing to pay (or accept) for an environmental quality change. As such, the emphasis of these techniques is mainly on their contribution to valuing *biological resources* as opposed to biodiversity *per se* (see Chapter 1). That is, they allow inference of values for, say, national parks or forest reserves, but the absence of direct enquiry restricts the extent of subject goods. Obtained values will be sufficient for cost-benefit purposes, but will rarely reflect less appropriable biological wealth. As such, the techniques provide only a lower bound estimate of the value of a particular biological resource.

The indirect group of techniques can be divided into two categories: surrogate market approaches and conventional market approaches.

Surrogate markets

Surrogate market techniques involve looking at markets for private goods and services which are related to the environmental commodities of concern. The goods or services bought and sold in these surrogate markets will often have as complements (or attributes) and substitutes the environmental commodities in question. Individuals reveal their preferences for both the private marketed good and the environmental good when purchasing the private good. They leave what is called a 'behavioural trail' as they make actual decisions that affect their lives. These techniques are therefore sometimes preferred by policy makers because they rely on actual choices rather than the hypothetical choices involved in the direct approaches. Surrogate market approaches include hedonic techniques and household production function techniques. The latter include the travel cost method which has been widely employed to detect the behavioural trail for biological resource preferences.

Household production functions

The household production function (HPF) approach argues that the environmental resource and private goods are demanded together with time, as intermediaries in a household's service flow or 'well-being' production process. The approach places values on environmental resources by specifying some familiar structural relations (restrictions) between the environmental services of interest and other private goods. In the HPF approach, expenditures on commodities that are *substitutes* or *complements* for the environmental characteristic are used to value changes in that environmental characteristic. Thus, noise insulation is a substitute for a reduction in noise at source; travel is a complement to the recreational experience at the recreation site (it is necessary to travel to experience the recreational benefit). The values of the environmental resource are found by looking at changes in the expenditure on goods that are substitutes or complements to the environmental resource.

The *travel cost approach* uses observed expenditures on the travel to recreational sites to estimate the benefit arising from the recreational experience. This approach has relevance for valuing ecotourism. It can also be used to value the benefits of forest and woodland conservation for fuelwood (using travel time as a measure of the value of the fuelwood), and similarly for water supply (using travel time as a proxy for the value of improved water supply facilities). The approach typically uses information on money and time spent by people in getting to a site to estimate willingness to pay for a site's facilities or characteristics. The problem here is that many recreation sites charge a zero or negligible price which means that it is not possible to estimate demand in the usual way. However, by looking at how different people respond to differences in money travel cost (including transport, admission and the value of time, etc) we can infer how they might respond to changes in entry price, since one acts as a surrogate price for the other and variation in these prices results in variation in consumption.

The travel cost demand function is interpreted as the derived demand for a site's services and depends on the ability of a site to provide the recreation activity. Only use values are therefore considered, with existence and option values being ignored. Since the recreation activity takes place at specific sites that have observable characteristics and measurable travel costs, then recreational service flows are described as site specific. The approach can therefore provide us with estimates of the value of the site itself and, by observing how visitation rates to a site change as the environmental quality of the site changes, provide us with values for environmental quality itself.

The travel cost approach makes the central assumption that visit costs can be taken as an indication of recreational value. However, if individuals have changed their place of residency so as to be close to a site then the price of a trip becomes endogenous and the central assumption is violated. The estimated demand curve will lie below the true demand curve and so consumer surplus will be underestimated. A similar challenge to the central assumption also arises in cases where the on-site time is not the only objective of the trip, eg where multi-purpose trips are made. The problem of multi-purpose trips presents particular problems for using the travel cost method to value internationally renowned sites which are typically visited as part of a wider experience. Several methods for allocating trip costs over all sites visited have been suggested (Mendelsohn et al, 1992), although none is considered ideal.

Data requirements: The data requirements of the approach are fairly substantial. A survey must be carried out to establish the number of visitors to a site, their place of origin, socioeconomic characteristics, the duration of the journey and time spent at the site, direct travel expenses, values placed on time by the respondent (see later), purpose of the visit other than visiting the site (multi-purpose visits raise problems for the technique), and a whole range of environmental quality attributes for the site and substitute sites (see the earlier discussion on environmental quality measures). All of this data collection is expensive and time consuming to carry out.

The socioeconomic characteristics will include things like income, age, a measure of education, sex, race, and perhaps some measure of the subjective strength of preference for the particular type of recreation being offered.

Time costs: Since the cost of visiting a site consists of the transportation costs plus the costs of the time taken to get to the site and the time spent at the site, the role of time is critical to the estimation of travel costs. Time costs are included because time has an opportunity cost, for example, one could work instead. We need to know what elements of time are to be included in the travel costs, what money values to use for these time costs, and how their inclusion will affect the demand and benefit estimates.

If time costs are ignored then benefits and demand will be biased, since, for example, two visitors to a site may have had to travel different distances to the site whilst having equal money travel costs but requiring substantially different times to get to the site. Unless time costs are included, visitation rates may appear to be equal for the two zones and willingness to pay for the site will be equal. The effects of both time costs and money travel costs on visitation rates therefore need to be estimated separately, but since the two may be highly correlated and so separate estimation difficult, time costs are given a money value using some shadow price of time and are lumped together with the transportation costs. Time at the site should also be included in travel costs because it may not be independent of the distance travelled. The shadow price of time at the site and time getting to the site may however be different. Any difference will be due to individuals deriving pleasure from the journey to the site, eg, by taking a scenic route. If no pleasure or displeasure is forthcoming then the shadow prices are the same.

The marginal wage rate is often used as an appropriate shadow price of time, since this reflects the opportunity cost of time between working and not working. However this trade-off may be distorted by institutional constraints such as maximum working hours, taxation etc; or, using the wage rate may be inappropriate for certain groups such as the unemployed. Previous empirical work has suggested that the shadow price of time may be substantially less than the wage rate and lie somewhere between 25 and 50 per cent of the wage rate with a value of 33 per cent of the wage rate being appropriate (Cesario, 1976). Some studies determine the proportion of the wage rate to use within the estimation procedure, eg Common (1973), McConnell and Strand (1981).

Exclusion of time costs in general will result in a more elastic (flatter) demand curve and bias the benefit estimates downwards. Exclusion of on-site time costs, if they are not independent of distance travelled and vary inversely with it, will result in a less elastic demand curve and an overestimate of benefits.

Specification and estimation issues: A trip-generating function estimating the number of visits to a site as a function of travel costs and the socioeconomic variables is the first step in specifying a demand relationship. Specification of the functional form is crucial to the benefit estimates obtained. Standard statistical techniques will in general not be able to discriminate in favour of one specification or another. In practice the choice of functional form needs to be determined empirically on an individual study basis. However a number of studies have found that the visitation rate equation is best estimated using a semi-log form, ie, the logarithm of the number of visits to the site is regressed against travel cost, etc. Generally, it has been found that log-linear and semi-log specifications increase valuations relative to results found using a semi-log for the explanatory variables (Smith and Kaoru, 1990).

The second stage in specifying the demand relationship involves explaining the variation in visitation rates across sites according to site characteristics. One procedure for doing this is to use the two stage varying parameter model of Smith and Desvousges (1986). Here, a trip-generating function is estimated separately for each site, without including any environmental quality variables as above. The second stage is then to explain the difference in the coefficients on the travel cost terms by regressing them on the environmental quality variables. The coefficient on the quality variable then shows how the demand curve shifts as quality of the site changes and thus can be used to estimate the benefits of a change. Using this second stage procedure also reduces the risk of multicollinearity problems especially where sites possess multiple environmental attributes which may be highly correlated. Inclusion of such attributes as separate variables in a single stage estimation will lead to multicollinearity.

There are a number of major statistical estimation problems with the travel cost approach:

1 Misspecification of the functional form can lead to biased parameter estimates.
2 The number of visits to a site can only be a non-negative variable such that continuous estimation techniques such as OLS are inappropriate. Discrete choice models of behaviour such as the multinomial logit model should therefore be used. This looks at the probability that a particular site will be visited, depending on the attributes of that site and other sites, and on the households' characteristics. Since individuals will make no visits to some of the sites then there will be some zero values for the visitation rate variable. Using OLS therefore implies that a change in the quality of a site will have an effect on visitation rates, even if the site is not visited. Clearly this is incorrect and so the logit model is used instead. In this, the benefit per visit of an improvement in site quality can be estimated from the logit equation if a measure of travel cost is included. An increase in quality will increase the probability of visiting a site. The benefit per visit is then found by calculating the compensating increase in travel cost that would leave the probability of visiting the site unchanged. This requires total differentiation of the logit equation. Use of such models also removes the problem of substitute sites, where individuals are faced with the choice of many sites at various distances and with different quality characteristics. Exclusion of the impact of substitute sites on demand will lead to biased estimates.
3 In any data set we will have information on people who actually have visited the site, but not on non-participants. Non-users need to be included to see what determines participation. This problem is known as *truncation bias* and has been found to have a significant impact on parameter estimates such that the estimated demand curve is flatter than the true one. One suggestion

has been to use *maximum likelihood estimation* instead of OLS in order to counter this problem. However the evidence here is mixed (see Smith and Desvousges, 1986; Kling,1987, 1988; and Smith, 1988). If there are systematic influences on the participation decision then a sample selection problem exists.

In conclusion, we can say the travel cost approach is an important method of evaluating the demand for recreational facilities. The techniques used have improved considerably since the earliest studies were carried out, both from an empirical and theoretical point of view. There are reservations as to its use, particularly concerning the large amounts of data required which are expensive to collect and process. Furthermore difficulties remain with the estimation and data analysis techniques and so the method is likely to work best when applied to the valuation of a single site, its characteristics and those of other sites remaining constant.

Whereas the travel cost method employed complementarity between market and environmental goods, the second HPF approach, the *averting behaviour technique*, makes a substitutability assumption. Examples of averting behaviour include: looking at expenditures on improved ventilation in order to reduce the exposure to radon in houses; valuing the costs of siltation from upstream erosion by looking at the expenses that farmers incur when installing protection structures; valuing health hazards from river water by looking at WTP for bottled water, filtration devices and private well installation.

To undertake such an estimation, data on the environmental change and its associated substitution effects are required. Fairly crude approximations can be found simply by looking at the change in expenditure on the substitute good arising as a result of some change in the environmental commodity of interest. Alternatively, if the marginal rate of substitution between the environmental commodity and the private good, which can be found from known or observed technical consumption data, is multiplied by the price of the substitute, then the value per unit change of the environmental good can be found.

Strictly speaking, in order to apply this approach the averting behaviour must be between two perfect substitutes, otherwise an underestimation of the benefits of the environmental good will occur. Averting behaviours are never likely to involve perfect substitutes and even when they do, bias in the estimation of benefits can still occur. For example, if there is an increase in environmental quality, the benefit of this change is given by the reduction in spending on the substitute market good required to keep the individual on their original level of welfare. However when the quality change takes place the individual will not reduce spending so as to stay on the original welfare level. There will have been an income effect as well as a substitution effect between environmental quality and the substitute good. Expenditure will therefore be reallocated among all goods with a positive income elasticity of demand and so the reduction in spending on the substitute for environmental quality will not capture all of the benefits of the increase in quality. Further problems with the approach include the fact that individuals may undertake more than one form of averting behaviour to any one environmental change, and, that the averting behaviour may prevent the adverse effects of reducing the environmental good but may also have other beneficial effects which are not considered explicitly, eg, sound insulation may also reduce heat loss from a home. Furthermore, averting behaviour is often not a continuous decision but rather a discrete one – a smoke alarm is either purchased or not, etc. In this case the technique will again give an underestimate of benefits unless discrete choice models for averting behaviour are used.

Thus, simple avertive behaviour models, although having relatively modest data requirements, can give incorrect estimates if they fail to incorporate the technical and behavioural alternatives to individuals' responses to quality changes. Although the technique has rarely been used, it is a potentially important source of valuation estimates since it gives theoretically correct estimates which are gained from actual expenditures and thus have high criterion validity.

Hedonic pricing
The hedonic pricing method (HPM) is similar to the household production function approach since both make a complementarity assumption. With HPM an attempt is made to estimate an *implicit price* for environmental attributes by looking at real markets in which those characteristics are effectively traded. Thus, 'clean air' and 'peace and quiet' are effectively traded in the property market since purchasers of houses and land do consider these environ-

mental dimensions as characteristics of property. The attribute 'risk' is traded in the labour market. High risk jobs may well have 'risk premia' in the wages to compensate for the risk. The two HPM markets of most interest, therefore, are:

- *Hedonic house (land) prices* – for valuing air quality, noise, neighbourhood features (parks etc). Given that different locations of property assets will have different levels of environmental attributes and that these attributes affect the stream of benefits from the property, then the variation in attributes will result in differences in property values (since property values are related to the stream of benefits) Ostensibly, land values in developing countries may well reflect the presence of soil conservation measures, access to fuelwood etc – characteristics favourable to the conservation of biological resources and incidental diversity. Similarly, property prices in developed countries frequently reflect surrounding aesthetic benefits of landscape or woodland. The hedonic price approach looks for any systematic differences in property values between locations and tries to separate out the effect of environmental quality on these values.

- *Wage risk premia* – for valuing changes in morbidity and mortality arising from environmental (and safety) hazards. Since labour markets in developing countries are unlikely to function so as to capture risk aversion, this approach currently has limited relevance in the developing country context. Note, however, that valuations from *developed* economies derived from wage risk studies may be adjusted to provide approximations of statistical life values for developing countries and economies in transition (Pearce, 1986).

To find the demand function relating the quantity of the environmental attribute to individuals' WTP it is necessary to first define the market commodity (eg housing) and the environmental attribute of the market commodity (eg air quality). A functional relationship is then specified between the market price and all the relevant attributes of the market commodity. This is called a *hedonic price function*. The hedonic price function is then estimated using multiple regression techniques from data on property values and the associated attributes of the property. We are thus able to find the hedonic price function coefficient on the attribute of interest (air quality) and this coefficient is known as the *marginal implicit price* of the attribute; it gives the additional amount of money that must be paid by an individual to buy an identical market good but with a higher level of the environmental attribute. Consider Figure 5.1. The analysis attempts to identify the slope of the curve AB, which shows the relationship between the level of air quality and the price of the property.

The curve AB in the diagram represents the result of a market equilibrium in which individuals buy property at some level of air quality and suppliers (owners or property developers) sell property with various air quality levels. The pollution level axis shows increasing levels of air quality. Individuals will buy property at some level of air quality according to their bid curves and suppliers supply property with this air quality level according to their offer curves, with points of tangency between the bid and offer curves giving equilibrium points on the hedonic price curve.

In benefit estimation we are interested in individuals' willingness to pay for better air quality. How does this relate to the following diagram? Well, say the level of air quality changes from q_1 to q_2, then individuals' willingness to pay for this change is given by the distance *ab* in the diagram. However, the estimated hedonic price function would tell us that the willingness to pay for the change

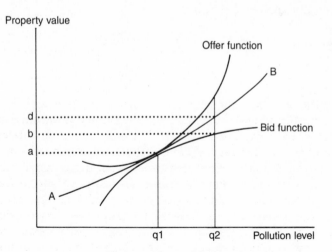

Figure 5.1 *The hedonic price curve*

would be the distance *ad*, and so gives an overestimate of the benefits of the change. To correct for this bias and so estimate the true inverse demand (willingness to pay) curve, a second stage to the procedure is used. This second stage of the analysis requires certain assumptions regarding the supply side of the market good in order to estimate the willingness to pay curve. This usually takes the form of a fixed supply assumption. A further statistical regression in which the marginal implicit price of air quality is regressed against the socioeconomic characteristics of individuals (including income) is undertaken to estimate the bid function.

This second stage of the analysis is not always necessary. Freeman (1979) shows that if all individuals are identical in all respects such as income, preferences, etc, then the implicit price function over the range of air quality (the slope of the hedonic price function over the air quality range) will give the inverse demand function since the implicit price function shows the locus of points on individuals' inverse demand curves which will all coincide since individuals have the same preferences, income and so on. Although this assumption allows easy benefit estimation from just the hedonic price function it is obviously a fairly unrealistic case.

Alternatively we can make various assumptions regarding the shape of the inverse demand curve in order to estimate the benefits of the quality change. These are considered highly questionable and so we do not analyse them further here.

Data requirements: The data requirements of the approach are substantial. Data from a wide range of different properties are required with information on all features that influence the properties' value such as structural characteristics (number of rooms, size, etc), neighbourhood characteristics ('prestige', closeness to business and amenity areas, etc), and environmental characteristics (air quality, noise levels, etc), as on the property values themselves. In practice, cross sectional data tend to be used. This removes problems regarding changes in the economic wellbeing of an area which will tend to arise if time series data are used. Socio-economic data on individuals (such as income, age, education, etc) are also required if the second stage estimation procedure is carried out. Sufficient data of the variety to enable reliable estimation may be difficult to come by, especially in areas and countries containing a large amount of public sector housing. Moreover, in developing countries such data are likely to be incomplete or non-existent even in urban areas. This suggests that the technique has little potential for valuing biological resources in remote areas with undeveloped asset price markets.

The data on property values should come from actual market data but since only a small percentage of the total owner-occupied housing stock may be sold per year, then collection of a large enough sample of data may be difficult. Care must be taken to account for the effects of property taxation on property values, otherwise their use will result in an overestimation of benefits. A further problem is that property prices may be influenced by expected future changes in the property, and so the characteristics at the time of a sale may not adequately explain the selling price. Rental price data could be used to overcome this and are in any case the theoretically correct measure to use. However the rental market may be even less perfect than the property market in some countries. As an alternative Real Estate agent valuations could be used.

A major problem with hedonic price studies is that of multi-collinearity – the fact that many of the explanatory variables will be related to one another, eg, sulphates and particulate measures will be collinear. This will result in difficulty in identifying which factor is determining movements in house prices. There are a number of ways to overcome multicollinearity. These include separating out the individual effects using statistical tests proposed by Klepper and Leamer (1984), or, formulating all data concerning individual pollutants into one proxy measure. Care must also be taken not to omit important explanatory variables as this will again bias the coefficient estimates.

Turning now to the data on environmental quality attributes, we need to know which pollutants are of interest and whether or not measures exist for them. Threshold levels may mean difficulty in measurement, or that pollution effects take a long time to show up. Temporal variations in concentrations may mean that it is best to use annual averages. We also face the same problems regarding objective and subjective measures of quality as we did for the travel cost approach. Subjective measures are what people's behaviour is based on and so are important for benefit estimation. Objective measures, however, are more extensively monitored for many pollutants. Will these objective measures coincide with people's perceptions? For measures such as suspended particulates which are readily perceptible and their effects apparent in terms of visibility, etc, there should be no problems. Sulphate pollution level measures are also thought to coincide with perceptions. When a single pollution variable is used, problems may arise with the pollution coefficient which may include the effects of omitted but collinear pollution variables.

Choice of functional form: The choice of functional form will have a significant impact on benefit estimates even if statistical tests find all the choices of form acceptable. In order for a preference to be made between functional forms, two questions should be asked about what properties the hedonic price function should possess. These are, whether the marginal implicit price of pollution is independent of the levels of the other attributes of housing and, whether the marginal implicit price depends on the pollution level itself, and if so, how? With regards to the first question only the log, and Box-Cox forms impose dependence on the levels of other attributes. The second question relates to the slope of the implicit price function and whether this is linear or not. In practice it is found that non-linear functional forms give better fits for the data, especially the log and semi-log variety. However, some studies use the Box-Cox transformation which allows the data to determine the precise form. Whichever functional form is used, care must be taken when transforming the estimated coefficients back to their original form (eg, from log back to antilog) since biases can result.

Other issues: The whole approach relies on the assumptions of a fixed supply of housing and a freely functioning and efficient property market. Individuals have perfect information and mobility such that they can buy the exact property and associated characteristics that they desire and so reveal their demand for environmental quality. In reality the housing market is unlikely to be so. As was mentioned earlier a large part of the housing stock may be in the public sector and so allocated subject to price controls. Furthermore market segmentation may exist whereby mobility between housing areas is restricted. To get around this problem separate hedonic price functions should be estimated for each segmented area. Mäler (1977) has criticized the fact that the technique implicitly assumes that households continually re-evaluate their choice of location.

Another problem with the approach is that hedonic price

includes the consumer valuation of not only present day benefits but also the stream of expected future (discounted) benefits from environmental quality, and as such will tend to overstate WTP.

Finally, the possibility that mitigating or averting behaviour by individuals may take place to avoid the effects of pollution, such as installing pollution filters, needs to be looked at (see the earlier section on averting behaviour). If this behaviour is unrelated to the characteristics of the property then it will reduce the value of the property and need not be measured separately. If changes do occur to the property then the value of the property will increase and so such changes need to be included in the hedonic equation.

To conclude, the hedonic approach is founded upon a sound theoretical base and is capable of producing valid estimates of benefits so long as individuals perceive environmental changes.

Both the HPM and HPF infer environmental prices from direct consumption of substitutes and complement goods. These prices are use values only and therefore understate total economic value of environmental goods. Data requirements for the HPF suggest that the technique is of limited value in the context of developing country biological resources.

CONVENTIONAL MARKET APPROACHES WHEN OUTPUT IS MEASURABLE

These approaches use market prices for the environmental service that is affected, or, if market prices are not an accurate guide to scarcity, then they may be adjusted by *shadow pricing*. Where environmental damage or improvement shows up in changes in the quantity or price of *marketed inputs* or outputs, the value of the change can be measured by changes in the total consumers' plus producers surplus. If the changes are small the monetary measure can be approximated by *market values*. Two approaches may be distinguished: the dose-response technique and the replacement cost approach.

The dose-response technique

This aims to establish a relationship between environmental damage (response) and some cause of the damage such as pollution (dose), such that a given level of pollution is associated with a change in output which is then valued at market, revealed/inferred, or shadow prices. Where individuals are unaware of the impact on utility of a change in environmental quality then direct WTP/WTA is an inappropriate measure and so dose-response procedures which do not rely on individuals' preferences can be used.

The technique is used extensively where dose-response relationships between some cause of damage such as pollution, and output/impacts are known. For example, it has been used to look at the effect of pollution on health, physical depreciation of material assets such as metal and buildings, aquatic ecosystems, vegetation and soil erosion. The approach is mainly applicable to environmental changes that have impacts on marketable goods and so it is unsuitable for valuing non-use benefits.

Damage actually done is found using a 'dose-response function' which relates physical/biological changes in the ambient environment to the level of the cause of the change. The dose-response function is then multiplied by the unit 'price' or value per unit of physical damage to give a 'monetary damage function'.

The dose-response approach in its most basic form looks at environmental resources which lead to a marginal change in the output of a good sold on a competitive market and values the impact directly in terms of output changes valued at market prices. More formally, suppose the production function for a single output y is given by:

$$y = F(X, Z)$$

where X is a set of inputs and Z is the input of the unpriced environmental resource. Assume that we can measure the output y and that this output is sold on a market at prices. The price of inputs X is given by the price vector P. Now, if prices are not expected to change when supply of the environmental resource changes, then the economic value of the change in the supply of the resource is the value of the production change accompanying the change in resource availability at constant inputs of the other factors.

If the change in resource supply is large, but leaves prices unchanged, then the value of the resource supply change must be measured as the difference between the profit after the change and before the change, taking all changes in factor use into consideration. If, on the other hand, the dose *does* cause prices to change (working through quantity) then there are still changes in profit, but there will be an additional effect on consumers' surplus. In other words the total welfare effect of the dose becomes difficult to determine particularly if resource producers take their own avertive steps to mitigate pollution effects.

In practice all these effects need to be assessed within the framework of a market model. Modelling welfare effects can be an open-ended activity depending on the desired degree of sophistication. To the extent that a model misspecifies the dose-response relationship and related market effects, measurement of welfare change may be biased. Specification of an accurate dose-response relationship is a particularly difficult task requiring precise experimental data and consideration of any synergistic effects between pollutants impacting on the subject receptor. Moreover, the potential presence of damage thresholds and response function discontinuities in ecosystems, suggests that simple linear dose-response relationships may be inadequate.

To conclude, the dose-response approach is a technique that can be used where the physical and ecological relationships between pollution and output or impact are known. The approach cannot estimate non-use values. The approach is theoretically sound, with any uncertainty residing mainly in the errors of the dose-response relationship, eg, are there threshold levels before damage occurs, or discontinuities in the dose damage function? It is necessary to allow for the fact that the behaviour of individuals may change in response to changes in the environment. If this is not possible, but the direction of any bias resulting is known, then this should be stated. The approach may be costly to undertake if large databases need to be manipulated in order to establish the relationships. If the dose-response functions already exist though, the method can be very inexpensive, with low time demands and yet provide reasonable first approximations to the true economic value measures.

In the context of biological resources, application to fisheries, forestry and agriculture are particularly appropriate. In these sectors, causes of mortality and morbidity are relatively well understood, and reliable market or shadow price information is normally available. Identification of *in situ* dose response functions for a range of species and ecosystems represents a challenge which ecologists are beginning to address with reference to the fate of indicator species such as amphibians, mosses and lichens

(Pechmann et al, 1991; Wyman, 1990). Subsequent translation into economic damages is, however, some way off.

The replacement cost technique

This technique looks at the cost of replacing or restoring a damaged asset to its original state and uses this cost as a measure of the benefit of restoration. The approach is widely used because it is easy to find estimates of such costs. The approach is correct where it is possible to argue that the remedial work must take place because of some other constraint such as a water quality standard. Under such a situation the costs of achieving that standard are a proxy for the benefits of reaching the standard, since society can be assumed as having sanctioned the cost by setting the standard. However, if the remedial cost is a measure of damage then the cost-benefit ratio of undertaking the remedial work will always be unitary. That is to say remedial costs are being used to measure remedial benefits. To say that the remedial work must be done implies that benefits exceed costs. Costs are then a lower bound of the true value of benefits. If, to pursue the water quality example, the standard has clearly been set without thought for costs, then using replacement costs as a measure of minimum benefits could be misleading.

Another situation where the replacement cost approach is valid would be where there is an overall constraint not to let environmental quality decline (sometimes called a 'sustainability constraint'). In these circumstances replacement costs might be allowable as a first approximation of benefits or damage. The so-called shadow project approach relies on such constraints. It argues that the cost of any project designed to restore an environment because of a sustainability constraint is then a minimum valuation of the damage done.

Information on replacement costs can be obtained from direct observation of actual spending on restoring damaged assets or from professional estimates of what it costs to restore the asset. It is assumed that the asset can be fully restored back to its original state. However some damage may not be fully perceived, or may arise in the long term, or may not be fully restorable. Benefits will therefore be underestimated. Another problem here is that restoration of damaged assets may have secondary benefits in addition to the benefits of restoration such that replacement costs will under-estimate total benefits.

The replacement cost approach is useful for estimating flood protection and water regulatory services supplied by forested watersheds which provide natural barrages. Other possible applications include the replacement of traditional medicines and the costs of crop insurance to replace natural insurance afforded by genetically diverse traditional cropping systems.

Opportunity cost
In the opportunity cost approach no direct attempt is made to value benefits. Instead, the benefits of the activity causing environmental deterioration – say, a housing development – are estimated in order to set a benchmark for what the environmental benefits *would have to be* for the development *not* to be worthwhile. Clearly, this is not a valuation technique but, properly handled, it can be a powerful approach to a form of judgmental valuation. It is used here to indicate the kinds of economic returns that must be secured by biodiversity use if such land uses are to be economically preferred to the alternative land use.

CHOICE OF VALUATION TECHNIQUE

A growing body of case studies is indicative of the appeal of valuation techniques as additional tools to guide the conservation of biological resources. The value of resource diversity is a relatively new concern and some methods will be more easily tailored for the purpose of value elicitation.

All of the valuation techniques outlined have strengths and weaknesses as we have seen, and the decision on which valuation technique to use for a particular application requires experience and judgement on the part of an analyst. There are, however, some general points to consider when making a choice.

First, the technique should be technically acceptable with respect to its validity and reliability (see the section on the contingent valuation method). Measures obtained from the technique should be consistent and accurate. Methods suffering random errors require reliability checks to judge their predictive capacity. Methods suffering non-random error contain bias problems, thereby reducing reliability and the validity of the measurement results.

Validity cannot be assessed solely on the basis of technique methodology but must be considered alongside practical predictive ability.

Reliability problems will occur if the sample size of the data is too small or a survey design is deficient. Reliability is closely related to bias which can vary depending on the good being looked at.

The hedonic pricing and travel cost approaches have weak validity since they assume the underlying theory is correct in order to generate results, whereas CVM can build in tests for reliability and validity. A more psychological approach can be taken with CVM, with direct psychometric testing of validity and reliability.

Second, the technique should be institutionally acceptable such that it fits into current decision making processes. There are differing views as to the acceptability of monetizing the environment.

Third, it is important to consider the needs of the user(s) of valuation studies who may prefer the use of one valuation technique over another. For example, estimates obtained from travel cost or hedonic property value models may be considered too theoretical or too complex. On the other hand it may be felt that contingent valuation estimates are too subjective and unreliable to support policy debate and discussion. The analyst carrying out policy work must be sensitive to such concerns. The technique should also be user friendly in terms of how easy or difficult it is to use in practice.

Fourthly, the financial cost of the study needs to be weighed against the value of the information gained.

Finally it should be remembered that it will often be possible to use more than one valuation technique and compare the results. The estimates of value obtained from all the methods described will be somewhat uncertain. If the analyst has multiple estimates, then they will have greater confidence in the magnitude of the value of the proposed change. Several of the valuation techniques typically use data from a household survey (eg, contingent valuation, travel cost model, and hedonic property value model). When the implementation of a valuation technique requires that primary data be collected with a household survey, it is often possible to design the survey to obtain the data necessary to undertake more than one valuation method.

6

VALUING BIODIVERSITY: ECONOMIC ESTIMATES

INTRODUCTION

Chapter 3 presented a decision rule for comparing the relative returns from the sustainable use of habitats with the opportunity cost. This decision rule was shown at two levels: that of the individual owner of the land, and that of the nation or the world as a whole. The former was used to explain how biodiversity loss can easily accompany everyday economic activity. The latter was used both to explain the kinds of values that are not captured by the individual when making land use decisions, and to suggest a rule for deciding how much biodiversity there should be. From that discussion it follows that if the divergence between national values and local private values is large, then the nation in question will have an interest in modifying market decisions to correct the relevant externalities. If the global values are additionally large, then there is yet a further reason to modify the private decisions of the landowner. In this case however it becomes important to determine whether these benefits accrue globally or disproportionately to the host or a limited group of states. In other words, which party has the greatest incentive to pay for the modification of landowners' decisions? What is being discussed is not the appropriation of the landowner's rights to his or her property, although that would be one extreme form of control. Rather it is the *provision of incentives designed to modify land use decisions*. The technical phrase is that we seek the *attenuation of property rights*, but preferably in such a way that the landowner in question is actually better off because of the control than without it. Instruments designed to serve these objectives such as tradeable development rights and land easements were suggested in Chapter 4. They are illustrative of the potential for mutual gain which underlies the philosophy of sustainable development – to have economic gains but not at the expense of the environment or, better still, to profit from environmental conservation.

Chapter 4 also showed that some biodiversity losses arise because of private gains that cannot be easily justified, eg the collection of subsidies for land clearance, intensive cultivation in the context of already existing overproduction, and so on. Here the issue is not one of making the landowner better off with the control: the original intervention itself has no real justification. Its removal will therefore be a cost to the private owner.

However, obeying an efficiency criterion for the sustainable use of land is not straightforward. Apart from the intrusion of government policy, the rule assumes that states and individuals can both recognize and realize a return from their resources. This in turn suggests a level of information which is often superior to that which exists in most countries. Indeed, if many population biologists are correct, many nations may never identify the majority of species and ecosystems they possess, still less attach indirect or non-use values to their use. In such circumstances, our decision rule is commonly reduced from a comparison of the total economic value to a simple trade-off of the direct use value versus the opportunity cost. *Biodiversity will be more prone to depletion when direct use values are not realized.*

Two issues therefore arise. First, how large are the unrealized benefits of conservation ? Second, how can institutions be changed so that land users secure these unrealized benefits? This two-part approach defines the approach for the rest of the book, namely to demonstrate the economic values of conservation *relative to* the returns from land development; and to construct mechanisms for the *appropriation* of those values. The following section critically reviews the literature on how these benefits have been demonstrated using economic techniques. We then assess two of the more contentious arguments for resource preservation: the appropriation of value from plant genetic resources for medicinal purposes, and briefly, the value of genetic resources to agriculture. Direct use, option and quasi-option values associated with unscreened genetic material are often invoked to support area preservation. Yet the global value of these uses remains largely unquantified. Finally we review one of the only quantifiable manifestations of global existence value, the debt-for-nature swap.

A REVIEW OF ENVIRONMENTAL CONSERVATION VALUES

Numerous studies exist on the kinds of economic value that can be realized through conservation. A collection of such values is documented in Tables 6.1 to 6.4. The estimates vary in the degree of sophistication and the extent of benefit valuation. Non-use benefit estimation for example, is more frequently attempted in developed countries than in developing countries, where benefit estimation is usually restricted to use values. In addition there has been no systematic coverage of ecosystems or regions, although certain systems – particularly tropical forests and wetlands – are more common subjects of study. Few studies attempt to identify separate components of total economic value although many contingent valuation studies are designed to determine use and non-use values.

Differences in applied methodologies and a shortage of illustrative studies for many areas handicap any reliable generalization on the basis of existing data. Some ballpark figures are nevertheless beginning to emerge. Forest carbon sequestration and valuation

Table 6.1a *Conversion ratios for varying discount rates*

To convert r in row to r in column, multiply by cell value	r = 4	r = 5	r = 7	r = 10
r = 4, t = 10		0.95	0.87	0.76
t = 20	1	0.92	0.78	0.63
t = 30		0.88	0.72	0.44
r = 5, t = 10	1.05		0.91	0.80
t = 20	1.09	1	0.85	0.68
t = 30	1.12		0.80	0.61
r = 7, t = 10	1.15	1.10		0.87
t = 20	1.28	1.18	1	0.80
t = 30	1.39	1.24		0.76
r = 10, t = 10	1.32	1.26	1.14	
t = 20	1.60	1.46	1.24	1
t = 30	1.83	1.63	1.32	

Table 6.1 Economic values – tropical forests

Value category:	Direct use	Indirect use	Non-use values option, quasi-option, bequest, existence	Total economic value	Benefit (sustainable use)/opportunity cost ratio
Ecosystem type: Tropical Forests Sources: 1 Peters, Gentry and Mendelsohn (1989). 2 Gutierrez and Pearce (1992) 3 Ruitenbeek (1989a) 4 Tobias and Mendelsohn (1991) 5 Pearce (1991d) 6 Schneider (1991) 7 Balick and Mendelsohn (1992)	1 Sustainable harvesting in 1 hectare of Peruvian Amazon (timber, fruit and latex $1987). Net present value $6820 (local market values) relative to a net revenue $1000 h⁻¹ from clear-felling which risks uncertain regeneration. $3184ha⁻¹ plantations for timber and pulpwood or $2960ha⁻¹ from cattle ranching. 2 Estimated contribution of direct use to Brazilian GNP $15b. 3 Medicinal/genetic net present value $7/ha over 126,000ha (park area) or 426,000ha (with the additional buffer zone). This represents a minimum expected genetic value. Estimates depend on i) the probability of an area yielding a drug base ii) the method of valuation iii) an assumed extent of rent capture by local authority. 4 Travel cost valuation of	3 Arising from sustained use of the Korup forest: – Existence of watershed functions affording protection to Nigerian and Cameroonian fisheries: NPV (£1989) £3.8m (approx $6.8m) or $54ha, assuming that the benefit starts to accrue in 2010 and beyond (2010 represents the time horizon by which the continued use of the forest resources – in the absence of protection – would start to exhaust resources. The imputed benefit stream therefore represents the continued existence of resources). An imputed value of the expected loss resulting from flooding from alternative land use from 2010 onwards: NPV of expected value of loss by 2040 is £1.6m ($2.84m) or $23ha. Soil fertility maintenance.	Lower bound option value may be inferred from the current market value or foreign exchange earning potential of plant based pharmaceuticals. Attempts to gauge existence values in other contexts, rely on CVM to report WTP/WTA. To date only one study relating directly to tropical forests is available (10), although this does not report any foreign (explicitly non-use) WTP. However (2) set the existence value for the Brazilian Amazon at $30b, calculated using an arbitrary WTP figure (observed from various CVM studies), aggregated across the OECD adult population. Donations to charitable funds may be one possibility to place CV evaluations in context; however dichotomy between	2 Brazilian Amazon: ($199/pa) Direct use 15bn Indirect 46bn Existence 30bn Total 91bn NPV (using Krutilla Fisher) $1296bn 10 CVM survey of villagers willingness to accept compensation (WTA), to forgo use benefits for the creation of the Mantadia National Park (Madagascar). Implicitly their valuation will reflect a total economic value of the resource forgone. The survey revealed a per household expected mean WTA of $108 per annum which is aggregated over the affected number of households	1 Implicit ratios of 6.82, 2.14 or 2.3 depending on alternative use, but subject to qualifications regarding local elasticity of demand for harvested forest products. Note that a similar exercise (12) in another area of Peruvian Amazon contradicts these estimates with a ratio of about 30 in favour of logging and rotation cropping. 2 Total present value $1296bn over 3.6bn hectares = $360/ha relative to a net revenue from clear felling of $1000/ha. The implied ratio of 0.36 will not be strictly representative since the calculation of total economic value is not necessarily based on the assumption of sustainable use. 4 Implied for Costa Rica

8 Pearce (1990a)

9 Watson (1988)

10 Kramer et al (1993)

11 Guttierez and Pearce (1992)

12 Pinedo-Vasquez et al (1992)

13 Solorzano and Guerrero (1988)

14 Schneider (1992)

15 Grimes et al (1993)

16 Pearce et al (1993)

tourist trips to Costa Rica's Monteverde Cloud Forest. Average visitor valuation $35 (1988), producing a present value for trips assuming constant flows of $2.5m, or extrapolating for foreign visitors $12.5m. This gives a value per hectare in the reserve of $1250 relative to the market price of local non-reserve land of $30–$100/ha.

7 Sustainable harvesting of medicinal plants in Belize (*local market values alone*) net present value $3327 per ha compared to $3184 from plantation forestry with rotation felling.

9 Forest production (Malaysia) $2455/ha compared to $217/ha from intensive agriculture.

3 Tourism value from the Korup $19/ha.

10 Annual value of fuelwood to Malagasy households about $39 per annum.

15 Valuation of sustainable non timber harvest from 3 one hectare plots in the Ecuadorian Amazon, average net present value for the sites of $2306.

Benefit imputed based on crop productivity decline from soil loss which would take effect from 2010 onwards (the without project scenario) NPV £532,000 ($958,000) or $8ha.

5 6 Valuing carbon sequestration; crediting standing forest with damage avoided from adverse climate change: $1.2b–$3.9b/year, depending on assumptions of:
i) Damage estimate per tonne carbon estimated range $5–13 tonne.
ii) amount released, itself dependent on assumptions of per hectare sequestration and annual deforestation rates.

8 14 Carbon storage $1300–5700ha/year.

11 Total carbon storage value Brazilian Amazon $46bn.

13 Rio Macho Preserve, Costa Rica. Evaluates the replacement cost in terms of water services and energy generation resulting from reserve conversion to agricultural use.

observed reason for giving and actual use of funds. Problem of identifying organizations involved uniquely in forest protection.

3 Value of debt-for-nature swaps may provide an approximation of a WTP reflecting a non-use value. Varying implicit valuation of different sites is reflected in the price paid by conservation bodies involved. Some swap transactions have aimed to preserve tropical forest ecosystems (see Chapter 6).

10 Foreign visitor's WTP for increased Lemur siting in the hypothetical Mantadia National Park (1991). Mean bid was $65 (conditional on seeing the same number of Lemurs actually seen in the Perinet Reserve where visitors were surveyed). At current visitation rates to Perinet, the new park would generate a total additional WTP of $253,500 pa. This amounts to a present value of $2.16 million discounting over 20 years at 10%.

amounts to a necessary one time compensation of approximately $673,000 using a 10% discount rate and a 20 year horizon.

16 Categorized annual non-market benefits of 51.5 million hectares of Mexican forest ($m):

Tourism	32.2
NTFP	na
Carbon	3788.3
Watershed protection	2.3
Option value	331.7
Existence value	60.2
Total	4214.8

Total should be regarded as a lower bound estimate.

12.5 which is the ratio of recreation value per hectare of protected area to the highest estimated price of land outside the park.

7 On the basis of local medicinal plant harvesting only, the implied ratio of 1.04.

9 Determination of market prices in this study is uncertain (ie world or local) implied ratio 11.3.

3 1.07 total project ratio or 1.94 from the perspective of Cameroon when indirect project adjustments are included. These include figures for project related aid flows and value for uncaptured genetic and watershed values.

13 Implied ratio of 2.

Table 6.2 *Economic values – wetlands*

Value category:	Direct use	Indirect use	Non-use values option, quasi-option, bequest, existence	Total economic value	Benefit (sustainable use)/opportunity cost ratio
Ecosystem type: Wetlands Sources: 1 Barbier, Adams and Kimmage (1991)	1 NPV per acre ($1990) from the preservation of the Hadejia-Jama'are floodplain, Nigeria. Agriculture 41 Fishing 15 Fuelwood 7 Discounted at 8%	1 Groundwater recharge function for surrounding areas, potentially measurable by either WTP or using costs of groundwater depletion on local agriculture – ie a *production function approach* – as a minimum benefit approximation.	Significant option values from future tourism, educational and scientific uses. Existence values of wetland wildlife probably high although no explicit studies exist.	7 Bintuni Bay mangrove ecosystem, Inan Jaya. NPV of whole system ($1991 discount rate 7.5%) $961–1495m of which direct-use probably $152–534m. This value does not account for the high *cultural value* placed on the bay by the Irarutu tribe (10).	1 Benefit/cost ratio expressed in terms of the relative benefits accruing from alternative water use: $45 per 1000m³ of water maintained in the floodplain as opposed to 4 cents per 1000m³ from diverted water.
2 Samples et al (1986b)	*Other floodplain benefits:* Livestock and grazing Non-timber forest products Tourism, Recreation (including hunting), Educational and scientific benefits (genetic and information value).	*Other important functions:* Flood control and storm protection can in theory be approximated estimating alternative preventative	2 Some non-use values for wildlife (CVM estimates) $1990/annum/person: brown bear, wolf, wolferine (Norway) 15.0 bald eagle (US) 12.4 emerald shiner 4.5 grizzly bear 18.5 bighom sheep 8.6 whooping crane 1.2 blue whale 9.3 bottlenose dolphin 7.0 California sea otter 8.1		4 From a similar analysis of the Ichkeul National Park, Tunisia, direct-use benefits amounted to $134 per 1000m³ compared to *negative* returns from diversionary use.
3 Costanza et al (1989)		expenditure or replacement costs for sea defences and dykes. In Malaysia the cost of rock escarpments to replace eroded mangrove fringe is typically around $300,000/ km ($1990) (11). The same study quotes a 1987 EC estimate of the 'inherent' value of mangrove protection to Guyana as $4bn, though there is no indication of how the figure is			
4 Thomas et al (1990)	3 Louisiana. WTP Present value at 8% ($1990) per acre. Commercial fishery 400 Fur trapping 190 Recreation 57 Storm protection 2400 Total 3047				Given the difficulty of generalizing with respect to alternative uses for wetland areas informative cost-benefit ratios are difficult to provide. Where non-use values have been inferred from costs of imposing or
5 Bergstrom et al (1990)	5 Louisiana. WTP Present value at 8% ($1990) per acre Recreation 103		9 Revealed WTP (CVM) for preservation benefits of blanket bog area in Scotland (1990) (once-and-for-all		
6 Thibodeau and Ostro (1981)					
7 Ruitenbeek (1991)					

8 Hamilton and Snedaker (eds) (1984)

9 Hanley and Craig (1991)

10 Van Diepen and Fiselier (1990)

11 Fiselier (1990a)

12 Danielson and Leitch (1986)

13 Turner and Brooke (1988)

14 McNeely and Dobias (1991)

15 Bennet and Reynolds (1993)

6 Charles River, Massachusetts. Present value ($1990) per acre at 8%.
Recreation 3400
Water supply 80,000

8 Present value per acre (at 8%) of Mangrove systems. Direct use from fisheries, forestry and recreation.
Trinidad $15,000
Fiji $11,000
Puerto Rico $13,000

15 Tentative estimates of mangrove timber production in Sarawak of $123,217 per annum.

derived.
Nutrient cycling will normally have a measurable effect on fishing and agricultural yields (in deltaic areas) the value of which might also be approximated by replacement expenditures on nutrients and compensating technologies.

14 Sustainable charcoal production from mangrove (Thailand) generates an annual national income of approx $22.4m. Net profits are nearly $4000/ha for forests with average productivity of 230m³/ha.

15 Marine fisheries maintenance worth $21.1 million per annum.

payment) Present value £164.68/ha (approx $296.50/ha) implicitly representing the discounted future stream of user and non-user benefits. As such the value is interpreted as an option value. (See Smith, 1987).

12 An average annual amount ($343/acre) paid (by the US Fish and Wildlife Service in 1980). to owners of Wetlands in Massachusetts for *preservation easements*, can be taken to represent a minimum option value for the ecosystem in an unaltered state. Similar conclusions could be inferred by looking at the average value of *management agreements* negotiated between conservation bodies and land owners in the UK. Such an *alternative cost approach* has revealed a value of £70/ha/per annum for coastal marshland.

agreeing land use constraints (the cost of which represents a discounted future benefit stream), the implicit cost-benefit ratio will normally be at least 1 because the compensatory payment from the recipient's perspective will have to be at least equal to the perceived opportunity cost.

Table 6.3 Economic values – rangelands

Value category:	Direct use	Indirect use	Non-use values option, quasi-option, bequest, existence	Total economic value	Benefit (sustainable use)/opportunity cost ratio
Ecosystem type: Rangelands (semi-arid) and Wilderness areas *Sources:* 1 Brown and Henry (1989) 2 Western and Thresher (1973) 3 Dobias (1988) 4 Child (1984) (1990) 5 Coulson (1991) 6 Dept of National Parks, Zimbabwe (1991) 7 Jansen (1990)	1 Wildlife tourism. Viewing value of elephants in Kenya $25m/per annum. The same study gives an indication of the extent of revenue forgone through sub-optimal park entrance pricing. A rough WTP survey revealed a potential consumer surplus as high as $25m/per annum (a sum almost 10 times the value of poached ivory exports and at least a 10% increase in actual expenditures). Since people were only asked their WTP to preserve elephants, consumer surplus for all wildlife viewing is presumably higher. 4 *Wildlife utilization:* Non-consumptive game viewing, lightly consumptive safari hunting and live animal trade, consumptive meat and hide production. *Zimbabwe illustrative examples:* Non-consumptive use: Direct and indirect income accruing to the Matusadona National Park (1991) US$10.3m, 66% of	*Indirect benefits from sustainable wildlife management.* *Distribution of benefits to local communities as a result of sustainable wildlife management schemes.* 7 The Nyaminyami Wildlife Management Trust, Zimbabwe channelled approx Z$198,000 (1989) of wildlife revenues into local projects for health, housing, education and recreation. In addition the project was able to compensate local farmers for any damage incurred and offer cropped wildlife products for sale locally at subsidized prices. Direct and indirect provision of employment. Improvements in local infrastructure and potential increases in land and property values. Significant saving in the	3 Beneficial use project for Khao Yai National Park surveyed user WTP for continued existence of elephants at approx $7. Under certain assumptions of population and park use, the option and existence value of Khao Yai to Thai residents (for elephant preservation) may be as high as $4.7m/year. The extent of existence values might be approximated from the value of *vicarious tourism* – the consumption of books, films and TV programmes – particularly in developed countries, or from observed *charitable donations* to organizations involved in wildlife preservation. More crudely we might extrapolate on the basis of WTP information of visitors to wildlife sites in substitute countries like Kenya. In 1990 56% of overnight		2 Ratio of wildlife tourism revenue per hectare ($40) to income from extensive pastoralism ($0.80) 50. This ratio has probably increased significantly due to increasing value added in tourism. 4 Ratio of value of wildlife production (Z$4.20/ha) to Cattle Ranching (Z$3.58/ha) in Zimbabwe 1.17. Calculation based on economic rates of return (as opposed to financial rates), and accounting for the relative environmental costs would in certain areas of the country produce ratios of between 2 and 5. 8 Provides Present values for returns from game viewing combined with some form of elephant cropping and for viewing alone in Botswana

Reference				
8 Barnes (1990)	which foreign currency (5). *Safari hunting.* Value for foreign visitors in 1990 US$9m of which, value of trophies US$4m (6).	hidden costs of land degradation and soil erosion arising from agricultural production in marginal areas.	visitors to wildlife areas in Zimbabwe were foreign, of which 26% originated in Europe or North America (approx 151,000 visitors). Assuming 50% of these visitors reveal a similar WTP *in addition* to entry fees (in much the same way as in (1) ie a $100 permit for elephant preservation), extra revenue generated might amount to $7.5m per annum.	(1989). The ratio of the former to the latter range from 2.63 to 1.8 (depending on whether a 5 or 15 year horizon is considered) demonstrating the earning potential of consumptive uses. Comparison with the economic rate of return from cattle production on a per hectare basis could show ratios similar to those in Zimbabwe.
9 Imber (1991)	*Consumptive value:* Zimbabwe estimates it makes $4.7m/annum from the sale of elephant goods and services, a return of $75/km² over approx 74,000km² of elephant habitat. The proportion attributed to sale of goods has fallen significantly since the imposition of an international ban on ivory sales.	The role of elephants as keystone species diversifying savannah and forest ecosystems.	9 CV study preserve the Kakadu Conservation Zone (from mining development) revealed that Australians were willing to pay A$124/annum for ten years to avoid a major impact scenario and A$53 to avoid the minor scenario. Extrapolated to the whole population produced a total WTP range of A$650m–$1520m or a present value at 5% of between A$1m/ha and A$2.3m/ha over 5000ha.	10,11 Implicit tourist use to opportunity cost ratio range 0.5–4.6
10 Norton-Griffiths and Southey (1993)	10 Reports an opportunity cost estimate for Kenyan protected areas. Forgone revenues average $34 per conserved hectare per annum. However (11) elaborating on (1) reports an expected mean WTP per day by tourists of $72 for park maintenance. Depending on the visitation scenario (number of days on safari) this translates to a per hectare consumer surplus range of $16–$157.	Value added retained in the host country consists of: net revenues accruing to: local airlines, tour operators, hotels, transport and cottage industries.		
11 Moran (1994)				

Table 6.4 *Economic values – marine systems*

Value category:	Direct use	Indirect use	Non-use values option, quasi-option, bequest, existence	Total economic value	Benefit (sustainable use)/opportunity cost ratio
Ecosystem type: Marine/Coastal systems, Heritage sites **Sources:** 1 Carter et al (1987) Hundloe (1990)	1 Estimating the socio-economic effect of the Crown of Thorns starfish on the Great Barrier Reef. A travel cost approach provided estimates of consumer surplus of A\$117.5m/ year for Australian visitors and A\$26.7m/year for international visitors. The study showed that tourism to the reef is valued (in NPV terms) over and above current expenditure levels by more than \$A1bn.				3 Cahuita National Park ratio 9.54*. 4 Ratio of total (direct and indirect) benefits to total cost 11.5*. * A conventionally assessed ratio rather than one based on opportunity cost.
2 de Groot (1992)	2 Total direct use valued at \$53/ ha/year, comprising (\$/ha/year): recreational use 45 food/nutrition 0.7 Raw materials for construction 5.2 Energy resources 1.5 Ornamental resources 0.4.	2 Estimates provided for the Galapagos National Park, Ecuador: \$/ha/year Maintenance of Biodiversity 4.9 Value of fish breeding (nursery function) 0.07 (applicable to 430,000ha of marine zone). Watershed and erosion prevention functions 0.3 (applicable to terrestrial area of 720,000ha).	2 Option value for the Galapagos National Park set arbitrarily at \$120/ha/ year which is the approximate sum of direct and indirect use values from the park. The uniqueness of the Galapagos ecosystem suggests that existence values are likely to be significant.	2 Total annual monetary returns from direct and indirect use approx \$120/ha. In present value terms this represents \$2400/ha (at 5% discount rate) or almost \$2.8bn for the entire study area.	
3 Marcondes (1981)	Biochemical and genetic resource values are also thought to be significant though no estimates are provided. Provision of employment directly or indirectly related to the National Park is a considerable benefit to the Galapagos economy (60% of	5 Describes a CV survey to value visibility improvements at the Grand Canyon (from reduced sulphur dioxide emissions). Mean bid (\$1990/person/year) \$27. A high level of familiarity may explain the high value respondents seem to have been willing to pay in this study (compared to bids for endangered species – see Table 5.3). Higher WTP bids in habitat valuation studies have	8 Reports a mean annual WTP estimate of \$27 for diving in the Bonaire Marine Park. At current visitation rates estimated consumer surplus is \$325,000.		
4 Posner et al (1981)					
5 Schulze et al (1983)					
6 Hausman, Leonard, McFadden (1992)					

7 Carson et al (1992)

8 Dixon et al (1993)

2500 workforce). Tourism is the most important activity, contributing an estimated $26.8m to the local economy.

3 A form of travel cost appraisal of the recreational value of the Cahuita National Park, Costa Rica. Consumer surplus estimates were derived from observed wage equivalent travel time net of transport costs multiplied over a visitor population. The resulting benefit-cost ratio demonstrated that the park is economically beneficial.

4 Conventional benefit-cost analysis of the Virgin Islands National Park, St Johns, identified significant direct and indirect benefits associated with the park, particularly tourist expenditure and the positive effect on land values in proximity to the designated area. Little information is available on the environmental effects of alternative land uses or the extent of visitors' consumer surplus. Total benefit ($1980) approx $8295/ha over approx 2820ha of National Park on St Johns.

6 Recreation demand study to value recreation use loss caused by the *Valdez* oil spill in Alaska; about $3.8m (1989).

generally revealed a preference for protection of a perceived array of benefits rather than for a targeted species. As with other CV studies the Grand Canyon case has been the subject of much debate, particularly with respect to the levels of information and framing (hypothetical) bias (see Schulze et al, 1981).

7 Estimate median per household WTP of $31 as a one-off amount to prevent future oil spills. Aggregating over affected households derives an estimate of $2.8 billion as the total lost passive-use values as a result of the *Exxon Valdez* oil spill.

has been extensively documented (Brown and Pearce, 1992). Similarly one review of 24 non-timber forest product valuation studies indicates a median value of about $50 per hectare per year, but with net values ranging between $1 and $420 (Godoy, Lubowski and Markandya, 1993). Clearly there is some scope for both harmonizing methodologies and deciding when a methodology is or is not suitably transferred between developed and developing countries. For the purpose of comparing estimates of similar species or ecosystem values, consistent data collection and analysis are vital for comparing like with like. Similarly, the compatibility of unmodified developed country methodologies for developing countries needs to be considered. Initial experience with contingent valuation and travel cost methods suggests that minimal modification is necessary for their application. Household surveys in rural areas, or sectors remote from the monetized economy present greater difficulties. One area for further research involves possible modification of economic techniques for use in conjunction with an established body of participatory and rapid rural appraisal methods. Contingent ranking exercises would, for example, be compatible with focus group or key informant interviews.

ISSUES ARISING FROM THE EMPIRICAL ESTIMATES

Tables 6.1 to 6.4 suggest a number of issues for discussion.

What is being valued?

So far we have used the term 'biodiversity' for the object of valuation. But it will be evident from Tables 6.1–6.4 that what these economic studies are measuring is the economic value of 'biological resources' rather than their diversity. The reality is that most of the studies relate to the value of biological resources. How far they are capturing diversity is difficult to assess. Those studies looking at the valuation of habitats (eg the Kakadu study) may well be capturing perceptions of diversity – ie valuations may be high simply because the area is known to be rich in diversity. Diversity valuation requires some idea of the WTP for the *range* of species and habitats rather than the specific biological resources they happen to support.

Valuing diversity as such will be far more complex. Contingent valuation approaches offer the most promise since individuals can be presented with different ranges of species/habitats to see which they prefer. But information will be paramount: many life scientists believe that this diversity is fundamental to human well-being. Others argue that we simply do not know what the functions of diversity are. As such, individuals may not be informed of the potential value of diversity. Travel cost and discrete choice studies might also be used for diversity valuation if it is possible to look at choices between alternatives that vary in their degree of diversity.

Transferability

The extent to which the various estimates can be transferred from one context to another is open to question. Many of the valuations are specific to the areas studied. For example, it is unlikely that values based on contingent valuation will be transferable. Those obtained by an assessment of the local market – eg for medicinal plants – will reflect supply and demand in that particular context. Those conditions will vary in other contexts.

A second problem of transferability arises in the context of generalizing values to wider areas. For example, the study by Peters, Gentry and Mendelsohn (1989) on returns to the sustainable use of land in Peru cannot be used to argue that such values are typical of *all* tropically forested sites, even in the same region. This is because (a) the values of the non-timber products in question will be related to the existence of a market place. The further from the market, the lower such values can be expected to be, and (b) the expansion of non-timber product supply across all feasible sites would result in price falls for the commodities in question. As it happens, the Peters et al estimates have been severely criticized. They are for the value of the *inventory* of non-timber products rather than the *sustainable flow* of products actually used. The latter might be only three per cent of the inventory value (Padoch and de Jong, 1989). This disparity highlights some of the serious methodological differences underlying the received view of non-timber product exploitation. Godoy, Lubowski and Markandya (1993), point out that such studies lack consistency in the examination of extraction costs, methods for ascertaining household uses, and, in determining the correct 'forest gate' or alternative shadow price to be assigned to marketable quantities. Indeed the whole exercise of valuation seems in most cases to have been an afterthought. Even more serious, is the observation of a singular lack of evidence that valuation estimates are compatible with sustainable extraction. Hall and Bawa (1993) discuss methods for assessing biological sustainability of plant extraction, but few studies attempt to gauge the sustainable hunting yields. In the absence of more detailed analysis therefore, sustainability of forest use is at best case specific. When extraction is known to be non-sustainable, this can be indicated in an appraisal by deduction of depletion premium from the value of forest products. This would depend on how long the present extraction can continue and on the discount rate (Godoy, Lubowski and Markandya, op cit).

Although fraught with difficulties, the issue of transferring benefit estimates is appealing. Avoidance of a full-blown benefit study may represent a considerable resource saving for funders and agencies implementing environmentally sensitive projects. In developed countries, such savings are motivating considerable interest in an analysis of appropriate conditions for transferring estimates, and the establishment of a 'values library' of off-the-shelf estimates (Boyle and Bergstrom, 1992).

BENEFITS TRANSFER

What are the necessary conditions for using the economic value of an environmental change at one site as a surrogate for a similar change elsewhere? Is it always necessary to initiate a new study in a project area to determine how the well-being of individuals is potentially affected by an environmental change?

Suppose that a development project would result in the destruction of a certain number of hectares of wetlands, and an analyst wished to estimate the economic value of the environmental losses associated with this proposed project. Rather than attempt to undertake a new study at the site of the proposed development, the analyst could identify previous studies that had estimated the economic value of wetlands, and then assume that the loss of a hectare of wetland at the proposed development site would be the same as (or similar to) this previous estimate. Such an approach has been termed 'benefit transfer' because the estimates of economic benefits are 'transferred' from a site where a study has already been done to the site of policy interest. The benefits transferred from the study site could have been measured using either the direct or indirect valuation techniques outlined above. More formally, suppose the willingness to pay of household i for a change from an initial environmental endowment Q_0 to an improved environmental endowment Q_1 is given by:

$$WTPi = f(Q_1 - Q_0, P_{own,i}, P_{sub,i}, S, E_i) \qquad (1)$$

where

P_{own} price of using the environmental resource ('own price')
P_{sub} price of substitutes for use of the environmental resource
S_i socioeconomic characteristics of household i

Benefit transfer requires three steps.

1   We must find (a) a study where this demand relationship has been estimated for an existing site; and (b) where values for Q_1, P_{own}, P_{sub}, and S exist at the new site that we wish to value;
2   We must determine the geographic area over which households will benefit from the change in environmental quality;
3   We must substitute the values of the independent variables for the households at the new site that is being valued into (1) to calculate the benefits to household i at the new site. Then the analyst must aggregate these estimates for all households affected in order to obtain the aggregate benefits at the site.

It is not necessary that an analyst be restricted to the use of just one site as the source of information to be transferred to the new site. Information could be obtained from several sites and summarized for transfer to the new site. For instance, in the example above the analyst could take the average estimate of the value of a hectare of wetland from existing studies. A more sophisticated approach would attempt to explain the determinants of variation in parameter estimates from existing study sites, and then use this model and values of the independent variables (the determinants of the variation) from the new site to estimate the benefits (value) at the new site. Such *meta analysis* techniques, which test consistency of valuation estimates using a data base of similar studies are a useful precursor to benefits transfer. The process does, however, require the availability of a bank of reliable estimates.

Most of the existing applications of benefit transfer methods in non-market valuation have attempted to estimate the recreational benefits of new projects or opportunities. The advantages of the approach are basically that estimates of economic benefits can be obtained more quickly and cheaply than if a new valuation study is attempted requiring primary data collection and often taking much time to complete.

There are three approaches to benefits transfer:

1 *Transferring mean unit values* – here we assume that the change in well-being experienced by the average individual at the existing sites is equivalent to that which will be experienced at the new site being valued. The previous studies are used to estimate the consumer surplus or average WTP of individuals engaged in, say, recreational activities of various kinds. These WTP values of a day spent by a person in a specific type of recreational activity at the existing sites are multiplied by the number of days of such activity forecast to change or occur at the new site as a result of the environmental change, to obtain an estimate of the aggregate economic benefits from the recreational activity at the new site.

Table 6.5 shows a summary of unit values of WTP for days spent in various recreational activities obtained from 287 existing studies. These unit values are the estimated amounts that individuals would be willing to pay over and above their current expenditures in order to ensure the continued availability of the resource for recreational use. Both travel cost models and the contingent valuation method were used to obtain these estimates.

The problem with this approach is that individuals at the new site, for a variety of reasons, may not value the recreational activities at the new site the same as the average individual at the existing sites studies on which the unit values are based. More sophisticated benefit transfers can instead be attempted as below.

2 *Transferring adjusted unit values* – here the mean unit values of the existing studies are adjusted before transferring to the new site. The unit values can either be adjusted for any biases that are thought to exist, or they can be adjusted in order to reflect better the conditions at the new site. Potential differences that should be looked for between the existing and new site are:

Table 6.5 *Net economic values per recreation day reported by TCM and CVM demand studies from 1968 to 1988, United States (third quarter 1987 dollars)*

Activity	Number of estimates	Mean	Median	Standard error of mean	95% confidence interval	Range ($)
Total	287	$33.95	$27.02	$ 1.67	$30.68– 37.22	3.91–219.65
Camping	18	19.50	18.92	2.03	15.52– 23.48	8.26– 34.89
Picnicking	7	17.33	12.82	5.08	7.37– 27.29	7.05– 46.69
Swimming	11	22.97	18.60	3.79	15.54– 30.40	7.05– 42.94
Sightseeing and off-road driving	6	20.29	19.72	3.73	12.98– 27.60	10.33– 31.84
Boating, motorized	5	31.56	25.67	10.36	11.25– 51.87	8.27– 68.65
Boating, nonmotorized	11	48.68	25.36	15.85	17.61– 79.75	10.26–183.36
Hiking	6	29.08	23.62	5.82	17.67– 10.49	15.71– 55.81
Wintersports	12	28.50	24.39	4.48	19.72– 37.28	11.27– 66.69
Resorts, cabins, and organized camps [a]	2	12.48				3.91– 19.93
Big game hunting	56	45.47	37.87	3.47	38.67– 52.27	19.81–142.40
Small game hunting	10	30.82	27.48	3.51	23.94– 37.70	18.72– 52.04
Migratory waterfowl hunting	17	35.64	25.27	5.87	24.13– 47.15	16.58–102.88
Cold water fishing	39	30.62	28.49	3.24	24.27– 36.97	10.07–118.12
Anadromous fishing [b]	9	54.01	46.24	11.01	32.43– 75.59	16.85–127.26
Warm water fishing	23	23.55	22.50	2.46	18.73– 28.87	8.13– 59.42
Salt water fishing	17	72.49	53.35	14.05	44.95–100.03	18.69–219.65
Nonconsumptive fish and wildlife	14	22.20	20.49	2.30	17.69– 26.71	5.27– 38.06
Wilderness	15	24.58	19.26	6.10	12.62– 36.54	8.72–106.26
Other recreation activities	9	18.82	16.06	3.65	11.67– 25.97	6.81– 43.39

[a] Resorts were 1.83% valued at $19.93 per day; seasonal and year-around cabins were 3.06% valued at $3.91 per day; and organized camps were 1.79% valued the same as camping. Estimated as roughly 5%.
[b] Anadromous fishing estimates included in cold water fishing.
Source: Walsh, R G, Johnson, D M and McKean J R (1992) 'Benefit Transfer of Outdoor Recreation Demand Studies, 1968–1988, *Water Resources Reserch*, vol 28, no 3, March (Special Section: Problems and Issues in the Validity of Benefit Transfer Methodologies).

— differences in socioeconomic characteristics of households;
— differences in the environmental change being looked at; and
— differences in the availability of substitute goods and services.

3 *Transferring the demand function* – instead of transferring adjusted or unadjusted unit values, the entire demand function estimated at existing sites could be transferred to the new site. More information is passed over in this way. As an example, for a zonal travel cost model, the demand function might be of the form (Loomis, 1992):

$$X_{ij}/POP_i = b_0 - b_1 C_{ij} + b_2\,Time_{ij} + b_3\,Psub_{ik} + b_4\,I_i + b_5\,Q_j$$
(2)

where

X_{ij}	number of trips from origin i to site j
POP_i	population of origin i
C_{ij}	travel costs from origin i to site j
$Psub_{ik}$	a measure of the cost and quality of substitute site k to people in origin i
I_i	average income in origin i
Q_j	quality of site j for recreational uses.

The approach requires that estimates of the parameters b_0, b_1, b_2, b_3, b_4, and b_5 are found from existing studies. Data is then collected on

1 population of zones 'around' the new site;
2 travel costs from these zones to the new site;
3 the cost and quality of the alternative recreational sites available to people living in the zones designated to be around the new site;
4 the average income of people in these zones; and
5 a measure of the quality of the new site for recreational uses.

The values of these independent variables from the policy site and the estimates of b_0, b_1, b_2, b_3, b_4, and b_5 from the study site would be replaced in the travel cost model (2), and this new equation could then be used to estimate both the number of trips from the designated zones to the new site and the average household willingness to pay for a visit to the new site (see Cicchetti, Fisher and Smith (1976) for an early example).

The use of benefit estimates is still in its infancy, and so procedures for dealing with problems common to most studies have not been standardized. Moreover, the paucity of valuation estimates in developing countries is such that value transfers could at best be international rather than on a (preferable) regional or local level. Additional socio-economic and cultural barriers to direct transfer of estimates are a further important qualification for any resulting appraisal. For the time being therefore, the practice outside countries with a sufficient bank of benefits research is likely to be restricted.

THE ECONOMIC VALUE OF MEDICINAL PLANTS

The potential pay-off from a 'blockbuster' drug provides a compelling argument for the identification and preservation of the world's most species rich ecosystems. Yet quantitative assessment of the likelihood of such returns is at best speculative, with some debate surrounding the merits of natural product screening relative to biotechnology and chemical synthesis. Plant species are used for medicines in two ways: (a) major commercial use, whether by prescription or over-the-counter sales, and (b) as traditional medicines which may or may not attract a market price. In the rich world, perhaps 25 per cent of all medical drugs are based on plants and plant derivatives. In the poor world the proportion is closer to 75 per cent (Principe, 1991). Clearly, both uses have an economic value, but what little work there is on the valuation of medicinal plants tends to focus on category (a). This should not obscure the likelihood that local willingness to pay for traditional medicines may be substantial. However, the difficulties encountered in accurately measuring the returns to local non-timber product uses apply equally to the investigation of ethnopharmacological uses. We therefore focus on the economic value of commercial drugs based on plants.

Substitution

While some medicinal plant resources have not been reproduced synthetically (*digitoxin*, for example), and others have been reproduced but are less efficient than the original material (synthetic vincristine from *Catharanthus* for example), many synthetic substitutes do exist. Two considerations are relevant. First, can biological diversity conservation be justified on the basis of the need for 'one off' exploitation before the material is synthesized, together with continued exploitation of plants which cannot be synthesized? Second, are future drugs more, or less likely to be manufactured from plant-based materials? The answer to the former question depends on the economic values that can actually be ascribed to the biodiversity resource, and on the answer to the second question. The answer to that appears to be uncertain. Principe (1989) reports on a UN International Trade Centre study which suggests that pharmaceutical companies have shown a decreasing interest in the development of new botanical products in favour of molecular biology and biotechnology applications to micro-organisms. Processing plant genetic material is time-consuming and expensive, and simple comparative rates of return are higher from other routes. On the other hand, others in the industry appear to believe that plant-based resources will re-emerge, facilitated by advances in screening processes, options for tapping into existing unexplored indigenous uses, and the potential to franchise out much of the screening process to host countries. This increased *in situ* capability appears to have been an important factor in the much-publicized prospecting agreement between Merck and the Costa Rican Instituto Nacional de Biodiversidad (Laird, 1993). Such agreements epitomize the potential for mutual gain and have focused considerable attention on the necessary national and international institutional requirements for maximizing returns to all parties.

Principe (1989) reports several reasons why research based on micro-organisms has limitations. The most important are (a) the steps of identifying the chemical structure required to achieve a given effect and creating a proper genetic code structure are the most difficult stages of drug development, and these are not helped by micro-organisms rather than plant-based genetic material, and (b) genetically engineered micro-organisms can, so far, substitute for only some of the plant-based chemicals. Indeed, Principe reports that the vast majority of plant-based chemicals have not been successfully synthesized.

The future of drug development may also be more, rather than less, dependent upon plant genetic material in light of the fact that plant-based research has gone in cycles. Findeisen (1991) reports that many thought that plant-based drug resources were exhausted in the early part of this century. The role of plants was, however, revived in the 1940s and 1950s with the discovery of the Vinca alkaloids (*Catharanthus rosea*) and reserpine (*Rauwolfia serpentina*). When the screening programmes at the National Cancer Institute and elsewhere in industry failed to come up with significant discoveries, the industry lost interest and screening programmes were effectively halted in the 1970s. The disinterest was compounded by the difficulties of plant-based drugs. The patent has to relate to the process of manufacture or to some unanticipated use value. Natural compounds *per se* cannot be patented. Thus, the Mexican government took control of Diosgenin resources in order to capture the rent from the production of *Dioscorea*, the main source of steroids in the early days of that drug. Attempts at the monopoly pricing of the resource forced pharmaceutical companies to search for synthetic substitutes. The case illustrates the problems of patenting and the problems facing countries that do seek to capture rents from biodiversity.

Some revival of interest in plant-based approaches in the last five years is accounted for by new techniques of purifying, analysing and assaying plant samples, including the use of robots for continuous assay of material. It is reported that among others, the National Cancer Institute, Monsanto, Smith Kline, Merck and Glaxo have revived plant screening programmes (Reid et al, 1993). Affymax and Shaman are new US companies developing drugs solely from natural products, and with a lot of emphasis on traditional medicines. The other main source of a revival in interest in medicinal plants is consumer demand for 'natural products'. Whilst consumers are unlikely to express a concern about the source material for major life saving drugs, they do express a significant concern about the sources of over-the-counter drugs and cosmetics, as the success of some natural products shops reveals.

Clearly then, medicinal plant values are relevant to use value arguments for conserving biological resources in the developing world. How far they have relevance in justifying conservation of biodiversity as such is more problematic. Some commercial sources doubt that genetic engineering of micro-organisms will totally displace plant-based research. This would suggest an insurance argument for conserving at least minimum diversity based on arguments related to the option and quasi-option values of the resource. These arguments are all the more powerful because of the extremely limited knowledge that exists about the medicinal properties of plants. But even here there are qualifications. There is not an equal likelihood that each species will generate a chemical suitable for manufacture into a beneficial drug. Some plants are simply more likely to contain the right genetic make-up than others. How far diversity needs to be protected to capture these option values is open to question. It may be feasible to focus on a 'genetic slice' of biodiversity and pay little attention to the broad spectrum of species. Offsetting this possibility is the argument that the genetic slice will itself depend for its existence and functioning on the broad diversity of species.

Evenson (1991) addresses this question to an extent. He distinguishes between two fundamental values of genetic resources as producer goods: one in the general strategic search for new resources which justifies the maintenance of most materials, and another in the specialized search for genetic material to meet specific needs, which justifies the collection and preservation of 'fringe' genetic resources. His calculations for rice suggest that if there is an economic case for maintaining an *ex situ* collection, the case for maintaining a near complete collection is stronger.

Overall, then, ascribing an economic value to medicinal plants can be done on two bases. The first relates to existing use values which, in turn, are for commercial drugs and for traditional medicine. The second relates to the *option value* of the plants, ie the extent to which conservation is required to protect *future use values*. Option values, in turn, are critically dependent upon the future of research in the medicinal drugs sector with respect to the base materials that are likely to be used.

THE ECONOMIC VALUE OF PLANT-BASED DRUGS

Ideally, what is required for economic valuation purposes is some idea of the ruling prices for plant genetic material and elasticities of demand by drug companies for that material. Given the availability of synthetic substitution as an alternative technology for some drugs, it seems clear that the demand elasticity will be high for those drugs, but fairly low for plant-based material that cannot, so far anyway, be synthesized. Drug companies today tend to use specialist plant gathering agencies (botanical gardens in the USA and a private company, Biotics, in the UK). In turn the gathering agencies use local institutions and people to engage in actual collection and shipping. Payment to the gathering companies is by contract or weight of material, but there are examples of agreements involving royalties in the event of successful exploitation. Thus, Biotics has royalty agreements with the companies it supplies and, in turn, those royalties are divided between the company and the source countries. To this end, these agreements already provide for the sharing of rents in the way clearly intended by the Rio Biodiversity Convention. Findeisen (1991) reports that royalties are usually negotiated on the basis of the value of the drug to the drug company, with royalty figures being in the range 5–20 per cent. But royalties are more readily negotiated for plant material to be used in a drug that is near to being marketed. Material that is destined for screening for longer term development is likely to attract low royalty agreements or simple one-off fees. Other companies have straight retainer agreements with botanical gardens and no royalty agreements. In the model used later, we therefore assume that a royalty rate of 5 per cent is applied to any plant material that results in the development of a successful drug.

Economic valuation to date has been fairly speculative but illustrative of the orders of magnitude involved. There are several ways in which to approach valuation:

- by looking at the actual market value of the plants when traded;
- by looking at the market value of the drugs of which they are the source material;
- by looking at the value of the drugs in terms of their life-saving properties, and using a value of a 'statistical life'.

If we do not take into account the prevailing institutional capability to capture the values in discoveries as implied in the last two points, the result will be exaggerated valuations for the host country. As Ruitenbeek (1989) notes, the economics of invention reveals that income realized by inventors is considerably less than the ultimate value to society of the product, because the traits associated with the ultimate products have a very low degree of appropriability. This is true with respect to the countries providing niches to the diverse flora and fauna where the discoveries have to be made. This aberration in rent appropriation becomes even more blurred when the assumptions of ignorance, uncertainty, essentiality, and substitutability about medicinal plants enter the analysis. This implies that a factor representing the institutional framework should be applied to the ex-post discovery valuation. This factor will depend on the existence of the licensing structure in the host countries; whether research conducted in the host country causes other leakages in the economy; and whether the ability exists domestically to carry out the research. Thus this factor is expected to be low in tropical low income economies. In Ruitenbeek's terms:

$$CPV = a.EPV$$

where CPV is capturable production value, EPV is expected production value, ie the patent value of one discovery. The fact that *a* tends to be low explains why developing nations feel that the benefit of their efforts to conserve biodiversity is captured more by others. That is, *a* can be thought of as a *coefficient of rent capture*. One purpose of the Rio Biodiversity Convention is to raise the value of *a*.

MODELLING THE ECONOMIC VALUE OF MEDICINAL PLANTS

We are now in a position to develop a simple model for determining the medicinal plant value of a unit of land as biodiversity support. The approach is fraught with difficulties given the considerable data deficiencies, but it is worth pursuing.

For any given area, say a hectare, there will be some probability, p, that the biodiversity 'supported' by that land will yield a successful drug D. Let the value of this drug be $V_i (D)$, where subscript i indicates one of two ways of estimating the value: the market price of the drug on the world market ($i = 1$), or the 'shadow' value of the drug which is determined by the number of lives that the drug saves and the value of a statistical life ($i = 2$). Since there are many other factors of production producing value in the drug, let r be the royalty that could be commanded if the host country could capture all the royalty value. Finally, let a be the coefficient of rent capture discussed previously. Then, the medicinal plant value of a hectare of 'biodiversity land' is:

$$V_{mp} (L) = p.r.a.V_i (D)$$

We consider each element of this equation in turn.

Probability of success – Principe (1991) estimates that the probability of any given plant species giving rise to a successful drug is between

1 in 10,000 and 1 in 1000. These estimates are based on discussions with drug company experts. Estimates of the number of plant species likely to be extinct in the next 50 years or so vary, but a figure of 60,000 is widely quoted (Raven, 1988). This suggests that somewhere between 6 and 60 of these species could have significant drug values. Put another way, if biodiversity use was favoured over alternative land uses, the realized benefit as far as medicinal drugs are concerned would be the economic value of these 6–60 species.

The royalty – Based on the observation that existing royalty agreements involve royalties of 5–20 per cent, but with a low figure for drug development some way into the future, we adopt a value of r = 0.05.

Rent capture – If host countries could capture rents perfectly then *a* = 1. Ruitenbeek (1989a) suggests that rent capture is likely to be as low as 10 per cent in low income countries. Hence a range for *a* is *a* = 0.1 to 1.0.

The value of drugs – Table 6.6 summarizes some estimates of the value of successful drugs. The method of valuation is important because it affects the size of the estimate significantly. The valuation based on life-saving properties gives the highest values, using the value of a 'statistical life' of $4 million (Pearce, Bann and Georgiou, 1992). Market values of plant-based drugs give lower values, and the actual traded price of the plant material the lowest value of all. The price of drugs reflects, of course, many more things than the cost of the plant source material. In that respect, the drug price grossly overstates the value of the plant. Equally, market prices understate true willingness to pay for drugs: there will be individuals who are willing to pay more than the market price for a given drug. Indeed, since the evidence suggests that such drugs tend to be price inelastic, this 'consumer surplus' element could be substantial. While there is no empirical basis for supposing that the consumer surplus element exactly offsets the overstatement in the price estimate, the two factors do work in opposite directions.

In the 1980s only about 40 plant species accounted for the plant-based prescribed drug sales in the USA. Thus, on the basis of prescription values only (see Table 6.6), each species was responsible for $11.7 billion/40 = $290 million on average. Since all life-saving drugs would be on prescription, use of the value of avoided

Table 6.6 *Some values of plant-based pharmaceuticals*

	USA	OECD	WORLD
	$ billion 1990 prices (bracketed numbers refer to the year to which the estimate relates)		
Market value of trade in medicinal plants	5.7 (1980)	17.2 (1981)	24.4? (1980)
Market or fixed value of plant-based drugs on prescription	11.7 (1985) 15.5 (1990)	35.1 (1985)	49.8? (1985)
Market value of prescription and over-the-counter plant-based drugs	19.8 (1985)	59.4 (1985)	84.3 (1985)
Value of plant-based drugs based on avoided deaths:			
anti-cancer only	120.0	360.0	
+ non cancers	240.0 (1985)	720.0 (1985)	

Notes: Ratio of OECD to USA taken to be 3.
'Value of a statistical life' taken to be $4 million in 1990 prices.
Lives saved taken to be 22,500–37,500 per annum in USA. Average is taken here, ie 30,000. Multiply OECD by 1.4 to get world estimates.
Source: Adapted with modifications from Principe (1989). See also Principe (1991).

deaths suggests a value per plant of $240 billion/40 = $6 billion per annum. Clearly some species were far more valuable than others, but taking the average it is possible to get some idea of the lost pharmaceutical value from disappearing species. If there are 60,000 species likely to be unavailable for medical research, and the probability that any given plant will produce a marketable prescription drug is 10^{-3} to 10^{-4} then, taking a mean of 5.10^{-4} and applying it to the 60,000 estimated losses means that 30 plant-based drugs will be lost from species reduction. On market-based figures, the *annual* loss to the USA alone would therefore be 30 × $292 million = $8.8 billion, and to OECD countries generally perhaps $25 billion. In an update, Principe (1991) suggests that USA 1990 prescription plant-based medicines had a retail value of $15.5 billion, which would raise the value per plant to $390 million. As a benchmark, the GNP produced in the whole of Brazilian Amazonia is some $18 billion per annum. On the 'value of life approach' the *annual* losses would be 30 × $6 billion = $180 billion for the USA, and over $500 billion for the OECD countries generally. However, these figures assume that substitutes would not be forthcoming in the event that the plant species did become extinct.

The value of land for medicinal plants

Using the previous estimates it is possible to arrive at an estimate of the value of a 'representative' hectare of land. The model can now be written:

$$V_{mp} (L) = \{N_R.p.r.a.\ V_i/n\}/H \text{ per annum}$$

where the new notation is:

N_R = number of plant species at risk
n = number of drugs based on plant species
H = number of hectares of land likely to support medicinal plants
and
N_R = 60,000
p = 1/10,000 to 1/1000
r = 0.05
a = 0.1 to 1
V/n = 0.39 to 7.00 billion US$
H = 1 billion hectares, the approximate area of tropical forest left in the world.

The resulting range of values is from $0.01 to $21 per hectare. If a = 1 at all times, then the range is $0.1 to $21 ha. Clearly, the lower end of the range is negligible, but the upper end of the range would, for a discount rate of 5 per cent and a long time horizon amount to a present value of some $420 ha.

Other estimates of medicinal plant values

Ruitenbeek (1989) suggests an annual value of $85,000 (£50,000) for a = 1 for the Korup rainforest. The relevant area is either 126,000 per hectare (the central protected area) or 426,000 ha (the central area plus the surrounding management area), so that per hectare values would be $0.2 to $0.7 per hectare per annum, very much in keeping with the lower end of the range obtained from our own model.

In a study of medicinal plant harvesting in Belize, Balick and Mendelsohn (1992) estimate the local willingness to pay for land. Their annual net revenues are $19–61 per hectare. These values are not directly comparable to the estimates obtained above since they relate to local medicinal plant use rather than the 'global' commercial values to the OECD countries. It is significant, however, that they just overlap the upper range of the global values obtained above ($21 per hectare). Note also that such local values would be quickly depressed if very large tracts of land were devoted to medicinal plants, whereas the global values obtained here would be fairly invariant with supply since the existing supply already has many features of an open access resource.

Overall, then, despite the formidable data problems and the difficulties involved, the model used here does suggest values in a range from very low to around $20 per hectare.

THE VALUE OF PLANT GENETIC RESOURCES FOR AGRICULTURE

Genetic and species diversity provide two important benefits to agriculture: a) the value of plant improvements and derived yield increases; b) a form of natural insurance against yield variability of homogenized systems. For conservation purposes, the issue is whether the value of these functions is maximized as the result of *in situ* genetic recombination, on farms and in the wild. If so, can mechanisms be devised for their capture? A related question concerns the distribution of benefits from the global adoption of new varieties originating in developing countries. The concept of 'farmers rights', first adopted by the UN Food and Agricultural Organization as part of an International Understanding on Plant Genetic Resources, is implicit in the terms of the Convention on Biodiversity. The concept recognizes an historically unrewarded contribution to crop improvement and the need for a framework for corresponding compensation. Whether these largely retrospective claims will be addressed with any accuracy remains to be seen.

Measurement of the benefits of germ plasm diversity to crop development is notoriously difficult (Evenson, 1991). The genetic resources are seldom traded in markets and common landraces are often the product of generations of informal innovations based on wild species. Accession to collections held by international agricultural research centres subject selected landraces to further human intervention. Identifying the contribution of an original landrace to the success of a particular modern variety is therefore a complex task. Furthermore, the base materials used for breeding are themselves the result of a production function which includes labour and on-farm technology. Unravelling the returns to respective factors with any degree of precision, including a return to all historical intellectual inputs is improbable. Compensation, if feasible, may only be determined on a geographical basis.

Literature on genetic resource valuation rarely notes a distinction between the commonly quantified returns to plant breeding research and adoption (see for example Bohn and Byerlee, 1993; Mooney, 1993), and the more complex identification of the returns to genetic materials net of complementary inputs. Netting out human and technological contributions to agricultural production is complex, since an accurate picture of the contribution of genetic resources requires assessment of the net incremental yield value at *every* stage of recombination. As it happens, information on parentage and genealogy of many common landraces is held by agricultural research centres worldwide. An accurate catalogue of yield effects of successive breeding stages and the necessary input cost information would require a much greater research investment. Cervigni (1993b) shows how a measure of the benefits of genetic material might be approximated in this way, using the difference between the benefits of an improved variety – commonly measured as the price multiplied by the yield increase – and the costs of all the other factors employed in breeding operations (capital labour etc). Data limitations mean that some degree of generalization of input cost information is inevitable. Costs and benefit streams arising in different periods imply some time discounting (see Annex at the end of this chapter).

Another method suggested by Evenson (1991) uses a methodology akin to hedonic pricing to relate yield value improvements to the genetic resources and other activities that were used to produce them. This approach may be particularly useful in revealing the relative contribution of genetic materials conserved *ex situ* to development of recent 'successful' varieties. The incidence of success would also be indicative of the returns to wild species collections compared to developments based on existing genetic materials.

The complexity of modern and traditional breeding practices means that only the broadest approximation of plant genetic value is possible, and then only for the most common crops. This uncertainty is reflected in estimates of the contribution of South germ plasm to the value of food production in the North (via crop research centres like CIMMYT – The International Maize and Wheat Improvement Centre). For wheat and maize only, estimates range from US$75 million per annum for Australia, $500 million per annum for the US and $2.7 billion per annum for all OECD states (Mooney,1993). It is not clear how much *ex situ* value-added is included in these estimates nor how they might be accurately assigned on a convenient per hectare basis to LDC agriculture. Such uncertainty should not be taken to imply that a vital global factor can remain unrewarded indefinitely.

GLOBAL VALUES: DEBT-FOR-NATURE SWAPS

Chapter 4 gave as examples of global values (a) the value of carbon storage in tropical forests and (b) the existence value attaching to biodiversity. This section looks at one possible way of uncovering the size of global existence values through 'debt-for-nature' swaps. Debt-for-nature swaps (DFNs) involve the purchase, usually by an international conservation organization, but also by governments and even individuals, of developing countries' secondary debt in the secondary debt market. Such secondary debt is sold by existing holders at a discount, reflecting the market's judgement on the probability of repayment. In a DFN, the holder then offers to give up the debt holding in exchange for an undertaking by the debtor country government or an acting conservation organization to protect a given area, train conservationists, etc.

The idea of valuing the biodiversity so conserved through DFNs is that the payment made reflects some kind of willingness to pay on the part of the conservation body purchasing the debt. Different DFNs can be expected to come up with different implicit valuations since the nature of the 'good' being bought will vary (eg the quality of the area protected will vary, and different packages of measures will be involved). Ruitenbeek (1992) has attempted to derive some WTP measures from six DFNs or deals which approximate DFNs. Here we outline the procedure used and show the implicit prices in a number of DFNs.

The basic idea behind a debt-for-nature swap is simple. If Y hectares of land are protected by a DFN costing the conserving agency \$Xm immediately, then the implicit price for a hectare of land is:

$$\$Xm/PV(Y)$$

where PV(Y) is the present value of the land expressed in hectares. The idea of a present value of a physical unit (as opposed to money) may not be familiar. Suppose the area protected is 50,000 hectares and the project is expected to last 10 years. Then, with a discount rate of, say, 6 per cent, the PV(L) is calculated as:

$$PV(L=50,000) = 50,000[d1 + d2 + d3...+d10]$$

where $d1 = 1/(1.06)$, $d2 = 1/(1.06)^2$, etc.

In the same way, the \$Xm should also be expressed as present value if disbursements are made over a period of time.

Numerous swaps have been agreed. Table 6.7 sets out the available information and computes the implicit prices. It is not possible to be precise with respect to the implicit prices since the swaps tend to cover not just protected areas but education and training as well. Moreover, each hectare of land does not secure the same degree of 'protection' and the same area may be covered by different swaps. We have also arbitrarily chosen a 10 year horizon in order to compute present values whereas the swaps in practice have variable levels of annual commitment.

Ignoring the outlier (Monteverde Cloud Forest, Cost Rica) the range of implicit values is from around one cent per hectare to just over four dollars per hectare. Ruitenbeek (1992) secures a range of some 18 cents to \$11 per hectare (ignoring Monteverde) but has several different areas for some of the swaps and he also computes a present value of outlays for the swaps. But either range is very small compared to the opportunity costs of protected land, although if these implicit prices mean anything they are capturing only part of the rich world's existence values for these assets. That is, the values reflect only part of the total economic value.

Finding a benchmark from such an analysis is hazardous but something of the order of \$5/ha seems appropriate.

Table 6.7 *Implicit willingness to pay (WTP) in debt-for-nature swaps*

Country	Month/Year	Payment (1990$)	Area m.ha PV	WTP/ha (1990$)	Notes
Bolivia[1]	8/87	112,000	12.00	0.01	1
Ecuador[2]	12/87	354,000}	22.0	0.06	2
	4/89	1,068,750}			
Costa Rica:[3]					
4 Parks }	2/88	918,000	1.15	0.80	3
	7/88	5,000,000			
	1/89	784,000			
	4/89[4]	3,500,000	0.81	4.32	4
La Amistad[5]	3/90	1,953,473	1.40	1.40	5
Monteverde[6]	1/91	360,000	0.014	25.70	6
Dominican Rep	3/90	116,400			
Guatemala	10/91	75,000			
Jamaica	11/91	300,000			
Philippines[7]	1/89	200,000}	9.86	0.06	7
	8/90	438,750}			
	2/92	5,000,000			
Madagascar[8]	7/89	950,000}	0.47	2.95	8
	8/90	445,891			
	1/91	59,377			9
Mexico[9]	2/91	180,000			10
Zambia[10]	8/89	454,000			
Poland	1/90	11,500*			
Nigeria[11]	1989	1,060,000	1.84	0.58	11
	7/91	64,788			

* unrelated to area purchase

Notes: A discount rate of 6 per cent is used, together with a time horizon of 10 years. The sum of discount factors for 10 years is then 7.36.

1   The Beni 'park' is 334,000 acres and the surrounding buffer zones are some 3.7 million acres, making 1.63 million *hectares* in all (1 hectare = 2.47 acres). 1.63 × 7.36 = 12 million hectares in present value terms.

2   Covers 6 areas: Cayembe Coca Reserve at 403,000 ha; Cotacachi-Cayapas at 204,000 ha; Sangay National park at 370,000 ha; Podocarpus National park at 146,280 ha; Cuyabeno Wildlife Reserve at 254,760 ha; Yasuni National Park – no area stated; Galapagos National park at 691,2000 ha; Pasochoa near Quito at 800 ha. The total without Yasuni is therefore 2.07 m ha. Inspection of maps suggests that Yasuni is about three times the area of Sangay, say 1 m ha. This would make the grand total some 3 m ha. The PV of this over 10 years is then 22 m ha. This is more than twice the comparable figure quoted in Ruitenbeek (1992).

3   Covers Corvocado at 41,788 ha; Guanacaste at 110,000 ha; Monteverde Cloud Forest at 3600 ha, to give 156,600 ha in all, or a present value of land area of 1.15 m ha. Initially, $5.4 m at face value, purchased for $912,000, revalued here to 1990 prices.

4   Guanacaste at 110,000 ha, to give a PV of 0.81 m ha.

5   La Amistad at 190,000 ha, to give a PV of 1.4 m ha.

6   Monteverde Cloud Forest at 2023 ha × 7.36 = 14,900 ha.

7   Area 'protected' is 5753 ha of St Paul Subterranean River National Park, and 1.33 m ha of El Nido National Marine Park. This gives a PV of land of 9.86 m.ha.

8   Focus on Adringitra and Marojejy reserves at 31,160 ha and 60,150 ha respectively. This gives a PV of 474,000 ha.

9   Covers four reserve areas: Zahamena, Midongy-Sud, Manongarivo and Namoroko.

10 Covers Kafue Flats and Bangweulu Wetlands.

11 Oban park, protecting 250,000 ha or 1.84 m ha in PV terms. See Ruitenbeek (1992).

ANNEX TO CHAPTER 6

The problem of discount rates

Chapter 6 reports various empirical estimates of the economic value of biodiversity use. One complication adding to the uncertainty of the estimates is the use of varying discount rates and time horizons in reported present value calculations. For example, consider a flow of benefits of equal amounts, B, every year for 10 years. Then the present value of this stream of benefits is:

$$B [d_o + d_1 + ... + d_{10}]$$

where $d_t = 1/(1+r)^t$, and r is the discount rate. Typical discount rates lie in the range 4–10 per cent. The higher the discount rate, the more the present is being favoured over the future. Indeed, this is the purpose of the discount rate.

Unfortunately, making adjustments to secure valuations at some consistent discount rate is not easy. Not only do the discount rates vary, but so too do assumed time horizons, and so does the distribution of benefits through time. If, for example, benefits are not at a constant rate per annum, then adjustments can only be made by reworking the original estimates.

For consistent time horizons and annual constant benefits, however, it is possible to suggest simple conversion ratios. These are shown in Table 6.1a for selected discount rates. It will be observed that the conversion ratios are very sensitive to assumed lifetimes. Note also that these ratios cannot be used if the aim is to go from one discount rate to another, and from one time horizon to another.

7

THE DEVELOPMENT ALTERNATIVE

THE MEANING OF DEVELOPMENT ALTERNATIVES

Chapter 4 showed that biodiversity will often be undervalued because its functions are not marketed. But it is also showed that there is a further bias: the value of the non-conservation use of land tends to be exaggerated through subsidies and other forms of support. This chapter looks at the underlying 'true' rate of return to 'development' uses of land.

The sustainable use of biodiversity is consistent with a number of alternative land uses. The focus is on sustainable uses of biodiversity, but may also be on preservation in the sense defined in Chapter 1. For tropical forest areas, for example, biodiversity is likely to be conserved if a sustainable forestry regime is in place and/ or if the forest is sustainably exploited for minor forest products such as rattan, rubber, honey, nuts etc. However, it cannot be assumed that minor forest product exploitation is necessarily consistent with biodiversity conservation: it is perfectly possible for forests to lose significant biodiversity if they are exploited unsustainably, for rattan for example. In the same way, a number of agricultural regimes may be sustainable and consistent with biodiversity conservation. Some shifting cultivation, for example, is consistent with a sustainable biodiversity.

Typically, sustainability will be consistent with limited exploitation of use values, and will be wholly consistent with the maximization of non-use values. The uses that *do* alter the biodiversity profile are permanent agriculture and ranching, clear-felling, and industrial/residential land use.

AGRICULTURAL VALUES

Crops

The main habitat-displacing activity in the developing world is agricultural expansion, where agriculture includes both crops and livestock. Table 7.1 illustrates the changes in land area in selected countries. The table shows clearly that major increases have occurred in the areas of cropland in South America, Oceania and Africa, and significant increases in pastureland have occurred in Central and South America. These broad aggregates conceal some major changes which are shown for selected separate countries. What, then, is the rate of return for agriculture?

Ideally, an answer to this question requires that we have some idea of farm budgets in which 'typical' returns and costs can be compared. Moreover, in terms of the benefits to the host nation, these costs and returns should be shadow priced to reflect the true

Table 7.1 *Rate of land conversion, late 1970s to late 1980s (percentage rate of increase)*

Region	Cropland	Pasture	Forest
Africa	4.4	−0.5	−3.6
N and C America	1.1	3.1	1.0
S America	10.9	4.1	−4.6
Asia	0.8	−0.3	−5.3
Europe	−1.3	−4.0	1.1
ex-USSR	−0.2	−0.6	1.7
Oceania	11.6	−3.1	−0.6
Country			
Burkina Faso	27.5	0.0	−8.2
Cote d'Ivoire	20.8	0.0	−24.1
Uganda	20.0	0.0	−8.1
Brazil	17.1	6.3	−4.2
Paraguay	46.7	32.6	−27.7
Suriname	53.4	11.1	0.3
Bangladesh	1.5	0.0	−10.4
Malaysia	2.5	0.0	−11.0
Pakistan	3.3	0.0	17.3

Source: World Resources Institute, *World Resources 1992–1993*, Oxford University Press, Oxford, 1992, Table 17.1

underlying value of the resources used up, and the benefits obtained.[1] In practice, such data are hard to come by on any systematic basis. In addition, the data should ideally be in a form that permits some kind of extrapolation of trends through time. Otherwise it is impossible to secure any impression of the sustainability of the returns to agriculture. Estimates of returns at a single point in time may well be accurate representations of the profitability of agriculture at that point of time. But, especially where low productivity land has been converted, that profitability may well be unsustainable.

Unfortunately, the data on comparative rates of return to agriculture are not in a form that permit generalized statements about the sustainability of agricultural rates of return. Indeed, they are generally not in a form that permits even very confident statements about 'static' returns. Various problems arise. In order to achieve some generalization it would be useful to speak of the profitability of individual agricultural products, but production cost data are rarely allocatable to individual products in any meaningful way (Brown and Goldin, 1992). Studies also vary in approach, making comparison difficult, and there is a general absence of time series (Goldin, 1990). Farm cost data do exist for OECD countries, but the situation for developing countries is that no reliable comparisons exist. Thus:

> Comparisons of costs, including those using engineering cost methodologies, require extensive comparable cost data. In the final analysis, it is the absence of these and the practically prohibitive data collection and measurement problems involved, which preclude a comprehensive analysis of relative costs embracing developing countries.
>
> (Brown and Goldin, 1991)

In the absence of cost data, one approach is simply to look at agricultural yields and value these at ruling border (world) prices

---

1 A shadow price is the true social opportunity cost of the resource or product. For example, if labour is unemployed, the opportunity cost of labour is very low: if it is not employed producing product X it would produce nothing. If there is zero output the opportunity cost is zero, or it is the value of leisure.

where appropriate.[2] The resulting figures will then be an upper bound to national profitability since costs will not have been deducted. National profitability relates to the true value of the returns to the nation, rather than the actual returns to the land user – see Chapter 3. There are, however, formidable problems with using this approach of valuing estimated average yields at border prices.

First, this approach will not capture the rate of return for subsistence agriculture. Second, the picture is heavily distorted by the existence of widespread subsidies and price support to agriculture. As Chapter 4 showed, the relevance of these distortions is that from the point of view of the agricultural producer the profit from agriculture includes the subsidies and price interventions. It is the comparison between the actual receipts of farmers and the conservation values that is relevant for actual choices. In terms of what is socially desirable, however, the correct comparison is between shadow priced net outputs from the alternative land uses. Table 7.2 illustrates the problem.

There are some data on both producer prices, border prices and the total receipts of farmers (Webb, Lopez and Penn, 1990). These might then be applied to data on yields. Table 7.3 presents some data for agricultural yields, border prices and revenues per hectare

Table 7.2 *Crop prices, farm receipts and border prices*

Example: Canadian Wheat

World price of wheat (1987):	C$185 per ton
Domestic product price	C$120 per ton
+ 'Policy transfers'	C$85 per ton
+ Income per ton	C$205 per ton

Canada priced wheat *below* border prices in 1987, subsidizing consumers and placing an initial burden on producers. Various mechanisms were then used to supplement farm incomes, ranging from direct payments (of about C$45 per ton) to fuel subsidies, marketing assistance, freight rate subsidies etc.

---

2 A border price reflects the value of output if the nation sells it abroad (exports) or uses the output to substitute for produce that would otherwise have to be imported. It therefore reflects the true opportunity cost of domestic output, and must be contrasted with the value of the output when measured at domestic market prices which are often below world prices.

Table 7.3 *Upper bound estimates of economic revenues per hectare from crop production in selected countries*

Country	Cereal yields (tonnes/ha)	Border prices local currency/tonne	US$	Shadow revenues US$/ha 1987
Wheat				
Argentina	2.26	195	91	206
Bangladesh	2.48	5017	164	407
Canada	2.20	185	139	306
Chile	3.69	27502	126	465
China	4.05	562	151	611
Egypt	5.25	113	89	467
India	1.86	1786	138	257
Japan	5.66	26640	184	1041
Nigeria	1.12	573	142	159
Pakistan	1.75	2625	153	268
Turkey	2.05	81015	95	195
USA	4.34	70	70	304
Rice				
Indonesia	3.71	316479	192	712
Kenya	1.72	4192	255	439
S Korea	5.93	217437	264	1565

Sources: Yields from FAO; border prices from Webb, Lopez and Penn (1990); exchange rates from World Bank (1991)

when valued at border prices. The data need to be treated with great caution given that they relate to national averages for yields across different types of crops, and that actual exchange rates have been used to standardize on the US$ whereas 'purchasing power parities' should be used. However, the results are indicative of the orders of magnitude. They suggest, for example, that sustainable land uses will need to achieve benefits of the order of (in each case less costs of production): $200–400 ha in South America; $250/ha in India-Pakistan; $300 in North America; $600 in China; $700 in Indonesia; perhaps $1000 in Japan and even $1500 in South Korea.

These figures ignore costs. That is, they are gross national receipts rather than net receipts. To obtain net receipts it is necessary to deduct costs of production. Unfortunately, such data are not generally available. None the less, it is possible to get some idea of the proportion of gross revenues accounted for by costs.

Alexandratos (1988) suggests that costs of 'off-farm' inputs account for the following broad proportions of agricultural revenues:

	1982/4 (%)	*2000 (%)*
93 developing countries:	24	27
Africa (SSA)	10	11
Near East/N.Asia	36	40
Asia (excl China)	24	28
Latin America	25	29
Low income countries (excl China)	22	25
Middle income countries	25	29

These proportions suggest that we might take 75 per cent of gross revenues as representing 'profit' in most developing countries, with the exceptions being 60 per cent for Near East/North Asia and 90 per cent for Sub-Saharan Africa. If so, the summary figures for the NPV of traditional development uses might be:

South America	$150-300/ha
India/Pakistan	$190/ha
North America	<$300/ha
China	$480/ha
Indonesia	$520/ha
Korea	$1100/ha

Of course, the figures probably still overstate the competition faced by sustainable uses. Further losses in biodiversity will arise from expansion of agricultural land into areas not yet converted. These are likely to be even less productive than already converted land, with the exception perhaps of tropically forested areas. Moreover, these are 'one off' annual values and not present values. The issue of the sustainability of production on still-to-be-converted land arises in this context.

Table 7.4 shows comparative rates of return to alternative land uses in Peru. There are considerable dangers in extrapolating the estimates in Table 7.4. They relate to one land area only and it is near to a town with a well developed local market, hence the economics of fruit and latex production are likely to be favourable relative to most of the Peruvian Rainforest. Moreover, if many plots were utilized in this way the market for forest products – such as nuts – would quickly become saturated with consequent effects on prices and rates of return. The analysis also assumes that there are

Table 7.4 *Comparative returns to alternative land uses in the Peruvian rainforest (Equitos)*

| | NPV at 5%, US$ per hectare | |
	Sustainable use	Clear-felling
Fruit and Latex	6330	1000
Selective Logging	490	
Total	6820	1000

Source: Peters, Gentry and Mendelsohn (1989)

no subsequent uses for the land after clear-felling, whereas in fact clear-felling is likely to be the precursor to 'nutrient mining' activities involving crops and, lastly, cattle ranching. From the forest dweller's perspective then, it is the sum of returns from this sequence which defines the comparison with sustainable options. Given that the latter are often mistakenly a quantified inventory rather than a sustainable flow, the figures should at best be regarded as upper bounds. In this case they suggest that sustainable uses may yield 6–7 times the benefit of non-sustainable uses. Swanson (1991) reports a factor of 12 for sustainable forest production in Malaysia compared to intensive agriculture on cleared land (present value/ha = $2455 compared to $217 ha).

Livestock

Deforestation for livestock production is a significant cause of biodiversity loss. In some cases deforestation is for livestock directly. In other cases, notably in the Amazon region, livestock may be part of a sequence of land uses ranging from timber to subsequent 'nutrient mining' (Schneider, 1990; 1991). Estimating the rate of return to livestock regimes is also complicated by the presence of elaborate subsidies in many cases. Browder (1988a; 1988b), Binswanger (1989), Hecht, Norgaard and Possio (1988), and Mahar (1989) have shown that much Brazil Amazon ranching yields negative rates of return which become positive incomes to ranchers because of subsidies. Thus, Hecht et al show internal rates of return to a corporation's 'own' resources (ie excluding resources provided by the government) to be 16–29 per cent depending on the escalation of land values, but nearly all rates of return are negative on the total value of society's resources in cattle ranching.

Schneider (1990) argues that such negative rates of return are not ubiquitous in the Amazon: many smaller ranches have been expanding without the benefit of subsidies. Unfortunately, apart from Browder's findings, detailed data on rates of return appear to be unavailable even for such a well studied area as the Amazon. But of course if rates of return to ranching are negative it is necessary only for sustainable uses to show zero or positive returns for it to be safely concluded that sustainable biodiversity use is the better land use.

Outside of tropical forests, livestock production clearly can and does secure positive rates of return. For Zimbabwe, Child (1984) reports cattle ranching returns of Z$3.6/ha, but this compares to Z$4.2/ha for wildlife ranching, suggesting that a sustainable use may already secure higher ERRs than traditional ranching even without adding in other benefits to sustainable use. Table 7.5 shows relative rates of return to alternative land uses in Botswana. Financial rates of return refer to the returns to the land user, but without any subsidies. Economic rates of return refer to the (shadow priced) returns to Botswana. It will be seen that cattle ranching actually has the lowest rate of return of the options considered (and may indeed have a rate of return below the cut-off rate of the social discount rate which should be at least 6 per cent).

Table 7.5 *Comparative rates of return to land use in Botswana*

| Land use | Internal rates of return (%) IRR | | Comment |
	Financial	Economic	
Group small scale game harvesting	21	28	biltong, skins, trophies
Ostrich farming	19	14	skin, feathers, meat
Crocodile farming	18	14	skins, tailmeat
Tourist lodge	18	35	
Safari hunting	16	45	<3% offtake
Game ranching	6	7	meat, hunting
Cattle ranching	5	na	

Source: Barnes and Pearce (1991)

FORESTRY VALUES

Land clearance for timber production is a second major cause of biodiversity loss. Evidence on the rates of return to forestry is surprisingly inexact. Table 7.6 reports some estimates for Indonesia in terms of per hectare values, and for Indonesia and other countries in terms of values per cubic metre roundwood equivalent. Taking yields as being in the range of 30–60 cubic metres per hectare (Vincent, 1990), the values shown are consistent with per hectare returns of $900–2500 per hectare. These results are broadly consistent with the other data shown, although it looks as if returns over $1500 ha are likely to rely on optimistic assumptions about yields.

Leslie (1987) argued strongly that sustainable natural management of tropical forests could only be made to pay if non-timber values were allowed for. Otherwise, clear-felling systems or 'selective' systems that ignore damage done by felling selected trees, would remain superior on financial grounds. Vincent (1990)

Table 7.6 *Rates of return to timber production*

| Forestry regime | NPV $/ha | | |
	Selective	Clear	Sawtimber
(a) *Indonesia 1986$*			
at 5%	2705	2690	na
at 6%	2409	2593	2165–2419
at 10%	2177	2553	2130–2278
(b) *Indonesia 1974$*		1479–1642 (actual)	
		1873–2257 (potential)	
		$rent per cubic metre	
	Logs	Sawnwood	Plywood
1983 prices			
(c) Indonesia	53	23	–24
(d) Sabah	30	18	na
(e) Philippines	34	49	–34
1979 prices			
(f) Ghana	28–79		

Sources: (a) Sedjo (1987); Pearce and Barbier (1987); (b) Ruzicka quoted in Gillis (1988a); (c) Gillis (1988a); (d) Gillis (1988b); note that Vincent (1990) regards Gillis's estimates of Sabah rents as being far too low, perhaps by a factor of three; (e) Boado (1988); (f) Gillis (1988c).

has reworked Leslie's case studies to suggest that sustainable management is in fact more feasible than Leslie suggested if timber is valued at stumpage values and allowance is made for rising real prices of hardwood timber. High cost low yield cases produce positive NPVs in a few cases and in most cases when low costs and high yields prevail. Vincent's analysis is also helpful for present purposes in indicating the highest NPV obtainable for Malaysian forests of around $230 per ha at a 6 per cent discount rate, about one tenth the NPVs shown in Table 7.6 for Indonesia. Note, however, that Vincent's analysis is for sustainable forestry, whereas the selective cutting referred to in Table 7.6 could be sustainable and consistent with conservation of biological diversity, but is more likely not to be. Vincent's highest return is $850 ha for a 4 per cent discount rate, high yields and low costs. Vincent's $230 is very broadly consistent with the Peters et al estimate of $490 per ha for Peruvian rainforest which is at a lower discount rate of 5 per cent.

In the developed world the use of subsidies of various kinds leads to wide divergencies in the private and social rates of return to forestry. Pearce (1992) shows that returns in the UK from timber sales alone result in economic rates of return below the UK government's cut-off discount rate of 6 per cent, but that 6 per cent can be achieved in selected areas if recreational benefits and carbon-fixing benefits are included. In the USA, various interventions are used to subsidize forestry (Boyd and Hyde, 1989) but data on rates of return appear difficult to come by.

Overall, the very limited data could be interpreted to suggest that *sustainable forestry* systems consistent with biodiversity conservation may yield NPVs for *timber* ranging from negative to $2–500 ha. Less sustainable systems appear to yield $1000–2500 ha. Clearly, the focus for sustainable systems has to be on non-timber products and functions.

ILLEGAL LAND USE

Much land use in the developing world tends to be illegal in the sense that the land is reserved for one or more uses and the actual use differs from these.[3] The costs of monitoring and policing pre-

---

3 We are not including here the occupation of open access land where existing rights are ill-defined, or not defined at all.

vent the lands from being used exclusively for their allocated purposes. In terms of the actual land use decision, illegal uses are important. Biodiversity is at risk if the illegal land use threatens it. In turn, land will be used illegally if the rate of return to illegal use is higher than the alternative rate of return available to the illegal user. That alternative rate of return may, for example, be waged labour. In so far as illegal users run risks of apprehension and punishment, it is reasonable to suppose that illegal uses will be pursued as long as the return from the illegal use exceeds the alternative wage rate plus the cost of the risk of being apprehended. In this sense, illegal land use must be seen as an economic activity.

Milner-Gulland and Leader-Williams (1992) show clearly how the economics of illegal use militates against biodiversity. A local poaching gang in Zambia could expect to take 20 trips in order to be sure of finding and killing an elephant, and perhaps nearly 10,000 trips before being sure of finding and killing a rhinoceros. For the ivory the local hunter could get a much lower price than the organized gang because of the need to sell to middlemen. The chances of being caught are known as is the fine for being caught (the fine plus the confiscation of ivory and horn). Milner-Gulland and Leader-Williams show that, given the fines, the probability of being caught, the revenues from the ivory, and the costs of the expedition, it did not pay local hunters to hunt elephant in the Luangwa Valley. But it did pay organized hunters to hunt since the ivory price was much higher for them, and there was a one in seven chance of finding a rhino whilst hunting for elephant (with an average take of 3.5 elephants per expedition). Converted to US$ the two calculations of net revenues are:

$$NR = P_i/e + P_h/r - C - p.F - p(P_i + P_h)$$

where P_i and P_h are the prices of ivory and rhino horn respectively, e and r are the probabilities of finding elephant and rhino, C is the cost of the expedition, p is the probability of being caught, F is the total fine.

For local hunters, per expedition:

$$NR = 0.05 \times 47 + neg - 2 - 0.05(175) - 0.05 \times 47 = -\$11$$

For organized hunters, per expedition:

$$NR = 450 \times 3.5 + 770/7 - 88 - 0.05\,(175) - 0.05(450 \times 3.5 + 770/7)$$
$$= \$1500.$$

The example shows that organized hunting pays handsomely, whereas local poaching does not. While the profit cannot be expressed 'per hectare' it is nonetheless clear that biodiversity-based land uses will, where poachable animals are present, have to incorporate costs of protection to prevent such profitable land uses.

SUMMARY AND CONCLUSIONS ON OPPORTUNITY COST

While the evidence is difficult to assemble and interpret, what is available suggests the following (see Table 7.7):

1   *Crop production* uses of land probably yield economic returns of the order of $150–300 ha in the developing world and the USA, but $350–600 ha in terms of the private financial rate of return (this allows for the rough estimates of costs). In Japan and some of the newly industrializing countries the difference between economic and financial returns is substantial, with economic

Table 7.7 Summary of returns to development uses

IRR	Crops	Livestock	Forestry	Wildlife	Illegal
Financial					
LDCs	350–600 $/ha	Low. 6% Botswana	> than economic returns due to subsidy	16–20% Botswana	Disorganized: low organized: high
USA	700 $/ha				
Japan S. Korea	12,000–14,000 $/ha				
Economic					
LDCs	150–300 $/ha; 600 $/ha China	Low. 7% Botswana	Sustainable 200–500. Unsustainable 1000–2500 $/ha	14–50% Botswana	
DCs	750 $/ha Japan		0–4% UK 2–6% UK with recreation and carbon		

Source: see text

rates of perhaps $750 ha and financial returns of $12–14,000 ha. These are per annum returns and are not NPVs. This picture conforms to the widely held view that explicit and hidden subsidies in the agricultural sector are substantial and seriously distort the way in which land is used (Pearce and Warford, 1992; Repetto, 1986; see also Chapter 4).

2 In the developing world, *livestock* presents an unattractive economic option, with low positive or negative rates of return in Amazonia and low positive returns in countries like Botswana and Zimbabwe. Financial rates of return are again higher because of subsidies and general support for the agricultural sector. Once again, the general picture of livestock sector distortions is confirmed (Pearce, Barbier and Markandya, 1990).

3 *Forestry* earns maybe $200–500 ha in NPV terms if the forestry is sustainable, but $1000–2500 in NPV terms for unsustainable forestry. Again, this fits the widely reported facts (Repetto, 1988; Repetto and Gillis, 1988).

4 *Illegal uses* have to be thought of as economic activities with which biodiversity use must compete (Swanson and Barbier, 1992).

8

CAPTURING GLOBAL ENVIRONMENTAL VALUE

THE GLOBAL ENVIRONMENT FACILITY

Chapter 3 showed that biodiversity fails to be conserved because local and global externalities exist. At the global level, one way of thinking of this is that the rich countries of the North should pay the poorer countries of the South for the external benefits of their biodiversity. In the textbook world of Chapter 4, such payments would be some amount equal to or less than the 'Willingness to Pay' of the rich world for these benefits. It was also seen that some of these WTPs could be substantial, notably the value for carbon storage. This might be several times the value of land in the developing world for agricultural development. Once again, it is important to stress that the purpose of such 'global bargains' is not to take over the land from existing landowners. Rather it is to attenuate property rights so that land is used sustainably. More-over, and critically important, such bargains can work to the mutual advantage of both sides. The developing country farmer, for example, could be better off with the trade than without it.

We turn to some of the possible bargains shortly. But it is important to note that the world has already established an 'official' financial mechanism for making such trades – the Global Environment Facility. Set up in 1991 for a pilot phase of three years to 1994, the GEF is now in its operational phase. Its purpose is to invest in the developing world in order to capture the *global environmental value* of investments, policies and capacity building. Its remit is to do this in the context of biodiversity, global warming, international waters and the ozone layer. Its actions on the ozone layer involve funding substitutes for chlorofluorocarbons (CFCs) and this it does by meeting the difference between the cost of the substitutes and the original cost of CFCs – the so-called *incremental cost*. Its activities 1991–94 in the areas of biodiversity and global warming took place outside the scope of the Rio Conventions which were not signed until 1992. From 1994 onwards it must act via the Conventions of which it is the interim financial mechanism. No international agreements exist on its activities in international waters.

It is important to understand that the GEF is not a development agency as such. It operates via many development projects, but it modifies them so that the technologies used are cleaner than they otherwise would have been. Its purpose is not development as such, but the capture of global environmental value – the value that comes from reducing the 'global bads' of climate change, biodiversity loss and ozone layer depletion.

This specific function shows up in the way the GEF decides how much to spend. It funds only the incremental cost of a project. For example, imagine a developing country would have burned coal for electricity, but that the option to burn more expensive gas is available. From a development perspective it is probably better to burn the coal since it is cheaper. Coal burning becomes the 'baseline' activity. But gas would be cleaner from an environmental point of view (it has lower carbon dioxide). So, the GEF would consider funding the difference in costs – the incremental cost. Its rule for intervention should therefore be that the global value obtained exceeds the incremental cost. Since global value is typically not expressed in money terms, the approach tends to be based on cost-effectiveness, eg $ per tonne of carbon emission avoided.

The carbon example is relevant to biodiversity because the GEF is at liberty to fund both afforestation projects and projects that avoid deforestation. Calculating the baseline and alternative profiles for carbon emissions is not easy, but it can be done. As far as biodiversity is directly concerned, incremental cost will consist of the difference in the costs of biodiversity conservation in the baseline and the cost of some intervention. Since biodiversity conservation is not a priority for many developing countries, the whole cost of some interventions will constitute incremental cost –

the baseline cost is effectively zero. But many countries have bio-diversity plans and these may make up the baseline.

Note the difference between the global warming interventions and the biodiversity cases. In the former case, no *extra* energy is supplied. A given amount that would have been supplied anyway is supplied in a different, cleaner way because of the GEF intervention. In the case of biodiversity it is not a matter of 'supplying' the same amount of biodiversity at a different cost, but of ensuring that *more* biodiversity is saved than otherwise would have been the case. As it happens, the interpretation of the terms of the Convention on Biodiversity may hinder implementation in the unambiguous way of the Framework Convention on Climate Change. Explicit reference to the global value of biodiversity and cost-effectiveness in ranking interventions are notably absent, and this may complicate the calculation of incremental costs and the potential for saving the largest amount of global diversity per dollar.

To date, the GEF has distributed about $1 billion of funding to developing countries. In 1994–6 it may distribute as much as $2 billion.

CREATING GLOBAL ENVIRONMENTAL MARKETS

There are several ways in which global appropriation failure can be corrected through creating global environmental markets (GEMs) which we introduced in Chapter 4. We distinguish between private and public ('official') ventures, and between those that are regulation-induced and those that are 'spontaneous market' initiatives. Public regulation-induced activity arises because of international agreements such as the Biodiversity and Climate Change Conventions. Table 7.1 sets out the resulting schema. The examples listed are dealt with more fully in Table 8.1.

REGULATION-INDUCED MARKETS

The first way in which markets are emerging is via the existence of regulations or anticipated regulations. In turn, these regulations are international and national but since implementation is always at the national level we can treat them together.

Table 8.1 *A schema for global environmental markets*

	Regulation-induced	Spontaneous market
Public/Official ventures	Examples: government to government measures under joint implementation provisions of the Rio treaties: Norway, Mexico, Poland, GEF	Example: Government involvement in market ventures: Swiss Green Export aid; debt-for-nature swaps
Private sector ventures	Examples: carbon offsets against carbon taxes and externality adders	Examples: purchase of exotic capital – Merck and Costa Rica

Government–government trades

An example of an international regulation is the Framework Climate Convention negotiated at Rio in 1992. Under the Convention each ratifying country will have an obligation to cut back on CO_2 emissions, but the Convention quite explicitly recognizes that it is often cheaper for one country to cut back on emissions *in* another country, besides making its own domestic effort to cut back. Similarly, it may be cheaper to create 'sinks' for CO_2 in another country compared to cutting back domestically (Barrett, 1993a, 1993b). This scope for 'carbon offsets' or 'joint implementation' is potentially large, and the first joint implementation agreement has already been agreed between Norway, Poland and Mexico, through the medium of the Global Environment Facility (GEF). Norway agreed to create additional financing (through the revenues from its own carbon tax) for GEF carbon-reducing projects in Mexico (energy efficient lighting) and Poland (converting from coal burning to natural gas) (GEF, 1992). The US Environmental Defence Fund is understood to be in the process (1993) of developing a reforestation project in Russia. The US Government announced the *Forest for the Future Initiative* (FFI) in January 1993 under which carbon offset agreements will be negotiated between the USA and several countries including Mexico, Russia, Guatemala, Indonesia and Papua New Guinea. The aim is for the US Environmental Protection Agency to broker deals involving the private sector.

As yet, the procedures for joint implementation under the Convention are not agreed and it is likely that more deals will develop once the ground rules have been established.

Private sector trades

The European Community Draft Directive on a carbon tax and other European legislation also provides an incentive to trade in this way, as does state regulation on pollution by electric utilities in the USA. While not strictly a private enterprise trade, in the Netherlands, the state electricity generating board (SEP) has established a non-profit making enterprise (FACE – Forests Absorbing Carbon dioxide Emissions) and is planning to invest in forest rehabilitation to absorb CO_2 in Czechoslovakia, Indonesia, Ecuador, Costa Rica and the Netherlands itself. The FACE Foundation already has a contract with *Innoprise* in Sabah, Malaysia, for the regeneration of degraded forest lands.

In the US case the offset deals are currently not *directly* linked to legislation, but several have occurred which are clearly a mix of anticipation of regulation and 'global good citizenship' (Newcombe and de Lucia, 1993). These include the New England Electric System's investment in carbon sequestration in Sabah, Malaysia, through the reduction of carbon waste from inefficient logging activities. The forest products enterprise is run by *Innoprise*. New England Electric estimate that some 300,000 to 600,000 tonnes of carbon (C) will be offset at a cost of below $2 tC. Rain Forest Alliance will assist in monitoring the project. New England Electric regard the *Innoprise* project as the first of a series aimed at assisting with the corporation's plan to reduce CO_2 emissions by 45 per cent by the year 2000. *PacifiCorp*, an electric utility in Oregon, is considering reforestation projects in the US, urban tree planting programmes in the US, and an international sequestration project (Dixon et al, 1993). Two pilot projects have been announced: (a) a rural reforestation project in Southern Oregon which funds planting subject to a constraint of no harvesting for 45–65 years, at an estimated cost of around $5 tC; and (b) an urban tree programme in Salt Lake City, Utah at a provisionally estimated cost of $15–30 tC sequestered. *Tenaska* Corporation is considering sequestration projects in the Russian boreal forests. Ultimately, some 20,000 hectares of forests may be created in the Saratov and Volgograd regions at a cost of $1–2 tC. Russian partners in the venture include the Russian Forest Service, the Ministry of Ecology and others.

While these investments are aimed at CO_2 reduction, sequestration clearly has the potential for generating joint benefits, ie for saving biodiversity as well through the recreation of habitats. Much depends here on the *nature* of the offset. If the aim is CO_2 fixation alone, there will be a temptation to invest in fast-growing species which could be to the detriment of biodiversity. It is important therefore to extend the offset concept so that larger credits are given for investments which produce joint biodiversity – CO_2 reduction benefits.

The US Energy Policy Act of 1992 requires the Energy Information Administration to develop guidelines for the establishment of a database on greenhouse gas offsets, together with an offset 'bank'. The Keystone Center in the USA is also establishing an interchange of information with a number of electric utilities to explore the issues involved in the establishing of offset deals.

GLOBAL GOOD CITIZENSHIP

Several offset deals appear to have been undertaken quite independently of legislation or anticipation of regulation. *Applied Energy Services* (AES) of Virginia has also undertaken sequestration investments in Guatemala (agroforestry) and Paraguay and is in the process of setting up another project in the Amazon basin. The Guatemala project is designed to offset emissions from a 1800 MW coal fired power plant being built in Uncasville, Connecticut. The intermediary for the project is the World Resources Institute and in Guatemala the implementing agency is CARE. The project involves tree planting by some 40,000 farm families. Carbon sequestration is estimated to be 15.5 m.tons of carbon. The $14 million cost includes $2 million contribution from AES; $1.2 million from the Government of Guatemala; $1.8 million from CARE, with the balance coming in kind from US AID and the Peace Corps. Note that the motivations for involvement vary. AES's involvement relates to its concern to offset CO_2 emissions, whereas other partners are concerned with the local development and environmental benefits the deal brings. Dixon et al (1993) report the sequestration cost as $9 tC overall, but inspection of the data suggests it may be less than this. $9 tC would be expensive for carbon sequestration alone, but there are other benefits from the scheme, including local economic benefits. In the Paraguay deal, AES is planning to advance money to the (US) Nature Conservancy for investment in some 57,000 ha of endangered tropical forest. AES expects to sequester some 13 million tC at around $1.5 per tC. Local benefits include eco-tourism, scientific research, recreation, agroforestry and watershed protection.

Table 8.2 *Private sector carbon offset deals*

Company	Project	Other participants	Million tC sequestered	Total cost $ million	$ tC sequestered
AES	Agroforestry Guatemala	US CARE, Govt of Guatemala	15–58 over 40 yrs	14	a) 0.5–2* b) 1–4 c) 9
AES	Agroforestry Paraguay	US Nature Conservancy, FMB	13 over 30 years	2	a) 0.2 b) 0.4 c) <1.5
NEES	Forestry, Malaysia	Rain Forest Alliance, COPEC	0.3–0.6, period not stated	0.45	a) na b) na c) <2
SEP	Reforestation, Malaysia	Innoprise	? over 25 years	1.3	a) na b) na c) na
Tenaska	Reforestation, Russia	Trexler, Min of Ecology, Russian Forest Service etc	0.5 over 25 years	0.5?	a) na b) na c) 1–2
PacifiCorp	Forestry, Oregon	Trexler	0.06 pa	0.1 pa	a) na b) na c) 5
PacifiCorp	Urban trees, Utah	Trexler, TreeUtah	?	0.1 pa	a) na b) na c) 15–30

Source: adapted from Dixon et al, 1993; and Bann, 1993.
Notes: a) assumes 10% discount rate applied to total cost to obtain an annuity which is then applied to carbon fixed per annum, assuming equal distribution of carbon sequestered over the time horizon indicated;
b) assumes 4% discount rate applied to costs;
c) cost per tC as reported in Dixon et al, 1993.
* Barrett (1993a) estimates the total cost of sequestration at $0.73 tC

Table 8.2 summarizes the private sector carbon offset deals to date (mid-1993).

'Exotic capital'

Financial transfers may take place without any regulatory 'push'. The consumer demand for green products has already resulted in companies deciding to invest in conservation either for direct profit or because of a mix of profit and conservation motives. *The Body Shop* is an illustration of the mixed motive, as is *Merck*'s royalty deal with Costa Rica for pharmaceutical plants and *Pro-Natura*'s expanding venture in marketing indigenous tropical forest products. There is, in other words, an incentive to purchase or lease 'exotic capital' in the same way as a company would buy or lease any other form of capital.

The deal between *Merck & co*, the world's largest pharmaceutical company, and *INBio* (the National Biodiversity Institute of Costa Rica) is already well documented and studied (Gámez et al, 1993; Sittenfield and Gámez, 1993; Blum, 1993). Under the agreement, *INBio* collects and processes plant, insect and soil samples in Costa Rica and supplies them to *Merck* for assessment. In return, *Merck* pays Costa Rica $1 million plus a share of any royalties should any successful drug be developed from the supplied material. The royalty agreement is reputed to be of the order of 1 per cent to 3 per cent and to be shared between *INBio* and the Costa Rican government. Patent rights to any successful drug would remain with *Merck*. Biodiversity is protected in two ways – by conferring commercial value of the biodiversity, and through the earmarking of some of the payments for the Ministry of Natural Resources.

How far is the *Merck-INBio* deal likely to be repeated ? Several caveats are in order to offset some of the enthusiasm over this single deal. First, Costa Rica is in the vanguard of biodiversity conservation, as its strong record in debt-for-nature swaps shows. Second, Costa Rica has a strong scientific base and a considerable degree of political stability. Both of these characteristics need to be present and their combination is not typical of that many developing countries. Third, the economic value of such deals is minimal *unless* the royalties are actually paid and that will mean success in developing drugs from the relevant genetic material. The chances of such developments are small – perhaps one in one to ten thousand of plants species screened (Pearce, Moran and Fripp, 1992; extrapolating from DiMasi et al, 1991). *INBio* has undertaken to supply 10,000 samples under the initial agreement. There is therefore a chance of one such drug being developed. But successful drugs could result in many hundreds of millions of dollars in revenues. Finally, there are two views on the extent to which deals of this kind could be given added impetus by the Biodiversity Convention. The Convention stresses the role of intellectual property rights in securing conservation and is sufficiently vaguely worded for there to be wide interpretation of its provisions. But it also appears to threaten stringent conditions concerning those rights and technology transfer and it remains to be seen how the relevant Protocols are worded. If so, parties to the Convention may find private deals being turned into overtly more political affairs with major constraints on what can be negotiated (Blum, 1993).

Other examples of direct deals on 'biodiversity prospecting' include California's *Shaman Pharmaceuticals* (Brazil and Argentina) and the UK's *Biotics Ltd* (general purchase and royalty deals), while Mexico and Indonesia are looking closely at the commercialization of biodiversity resources.

The demand for direct investment in conservation is not confined to the private sector. The demand for conservation by NGOs is revealed through debt-for-nature swaps, which are further examples of these exotic capital trades – see Chapter 5 and Deacon and Murphy (1992).

Buying down private risk

Newcombe and de Lucia (1993) have drawn attention to another potentially very large private trade which has global environmental benefits. Investment by the private sector in the developing world is invariably constrained by risk factors such as exchange rate risks, repayment risks, political risks and so on. In so far as this investment benefits the global environment, as with, say, the development of natural gas to displace coal, the existence of the risks reduces the flow of investment and hence the global environmental benefits. But these risks might be shared ('bought down') by having an international agency, such as the Global Environment Facility, provide some funds or services which help reduce the risk. Given the scale of private investment flows, the potential here is enormous. Nor is there any reason why it should not benefit biodiversity, either indirectly as a joint benefit of other investments in, for example, raising agricultural productivity and hence in reducing the pressure for land degradation, or directly through afforestation schemes.

9

SUMMARY AND CONCLUSIONS

USE AND NON-USE ECONOMIC VALUES

Throughout we have taken phrases such as 'investment in protection' to mean either outright protection (non-use or extremely limited use) of an area or a focus on sustainable uses of the biological resources of an area – what we have referred to as the *sustainable use of biodiversity.*

Non-use is consistent with the appropriation of existence values, a willingness to pay for an area to be protected even though those who make the payment make no active use of the area for tourism or other products. In turn, existence values underlie some current or projected resource transfers under the UNCED Convention on Biodiversity and the current mechanism for which is the Global Environment Facility (GEF). Because the GEF is likely to be expanded in scope and resources we have devoted some attention to the benefits of non-use. However, our survey (Chapter 6) shows that we have hardly any examples of the measurement of existence values outside focused studies in the developed world. We considered debt-for-nature swaps as one mechanism whereby we could uncover existence values. Our analysis suggests an existence value of perhaps $5 per hectare on average, but we cite this number with some hesitation given the problems of eliciting values in this manner. Clearly there is a major gap in our knowledge with the absence of measures of existence value for the world's protected areas, especially protected areas in the developing world.

Because of the absence of existence value estimates, we have focused more on sustainable direct and indirect use values from biodiversity. Again, we note a marked difference in our understanding of direct and indirect use values. Direct use values include such things as eco-tourism, exploitation of genetic material for pharmaceuticals and crop breeding, the consumption of 'minor' forest products such as nuts, rattan etc, sustainable forestry and so on. There is an expanding literature on such economic values and we offer some broad conclusions later. We have found very little on indirect use values which can be reported in any credible, quantitative fashion. The exception is carbon sequestration for tropical forests. If global warming is a real phenomenon, then we estimate the implicit economic value of conserved tropical forests to be substantial and in the range $1000–4000 per hectare, which is often higher than direct use values that involve forest destruction (clearfelling for timber, agriculture, ranching), depending on location and circumstance. But carbon sequestration is not a priority for developing countries. Hence the argument is relevant to the kinds of resource transfer that the GEF should consider, or which might be the subject of certain bilateral deals of a 'debt-for-sustainable development' kind. That is, global values of the kind typified by carbon sequestration are relevant only if the issue of appropriability is resolved. We therefore highlight the limited amount of economic analysis available on the indirect use values of protected areas and urge that much greater effort be made to understand and elicit these economic values.

COMPARING DEVELOPMENT AND CONSERVATION

The economic approach to determining investment in protected areas requires a comparison of the 'rate of return' from protection with the rate of return from the alternative use of the land (or water) area. These rates of return may be expressed as such, ie in percentage terms, or as 'net present values'. In each case the benefits and costs over time are 'collapsed' to a single number (or a range if there is uncertainty about the numbers). We can now state the guidelines for comparing development and conservation in terms of basic economic rules:

> *The fundamental rule for investment in land use is that the return from any particular land use must be compared with the return from the alternative land use.*

While this may seem an obvious guideline, it is in fact ignored on an extensive basis. For example, if a land area is to be conserved, it is important to know what the local people and the nation at large must sacrifice by way of forgone agricultural output, timber etc. Similarly, if an area is to be converted from wetland to grazing, or forest to crops, it is important to know what benefits from conservation will be lost. Rule 1 may be summarized by saying that, on all occasions, it is important to compare the benefits and costs of development (Bd and Cd) with the benefits and costs of conservation (Bc and Cc). Conservation is justified in prima facie terms if:

$$[Bc - Cc] > [Bd - Cd]$$

From the perspective of the nation as a whole it is very important to value the benefits and costs net of all economic distortions in the market place, and to measure, as far as possible, gains and losses which are not reflected in any market.

Chapter 7 revealed a critically important issue, namely that sustainable land use ought to be competing (in terms of economic values) with rates of return to alternative land uses net of any subsidy or other form of hidden protection for that land use. But in practice sustainable land use has to compete with rates of return to individual land users which are grossly distorted through the use of tax breaks, subsidies, price controls and property rights measures. As an example, the prices received by farmers for agricultural produce in many countries are several times the price that the same produce would fetch if traded on the open international market. This inflates the private rate of return to farmers and means that sustainable land uses cannot begin to compete in the actual market place.

Unless these economic distortions are removed, the pressure to develop land for uses that are inconsistent with sustaining biodiversity will be so great that the conservation policies will themselves risk failure. Where investment in sustainable biodiversity use is afforded high priority, it will be essential to couple that investment with pressure to reduce and remove the land use distortions.

Investment should take place in biodiversity in a context where the local community gains most relative to other groups in society, and, at the very least, there should be net gains to the local community. No

> *investment should take place unless there are mechanisms in place for sustaining that investment. Local involvement is thus a 'sustainability' requirement.*

We found comparatively little information on the quantitative rates of return from different land uses to different groups in society. As an instance of the kind of information needed, it is reported that Brazil nut collectors in Amazonia collect only 3 per cent of the New York wholesale price (Tickell, 1992), suggesting a low local rate of return to this land use. In Kenya, frequently ineffectual revenue sharing schemes return only a fraction of measured visitors' consumer surplus to local communities (Moran, 1994). Similar observations apply to many uses of converted habitat – in Zaire for example, the top 1 per cent of the farmers cover 40 per cent of the land (Gradwohl and Greenberg, 1988). The idea of biasing investments so that their distributional impact favours the local community is more than an issue of equity or fairness. It is an issue of efficiency because, unless the local community secures net benefits from the investment, it will have no incentive to sustain the investment. The incentive will remain for the local community to encroach on the protected area and to develop alternative uses which do secure higher local gains.

> *Due account needs to be taken of the longer term benefits from protection. This may involve adjustments to discount rates but is more likely to involve some more direct reflection of long-term benefits in the valuation process.*

The way in which time is integrated into investment decisions is through the discount rate. High discount rates tend to favour short-term benefits. This affects the comparison of sustainable land uses with alternative land uses since alternative land uses, eg crop growing or ranching on deforested land, may often amount to the 'mining' of the land for its nutrients. If the discount rate is high, the mining option can easily be favoured over the sustainable use option since the latter explicitly speaks of sustainable uses and hence long-lasting uses of the land.

Our survey of the economic returns to sustainable land use and returns to alternative land uses suggest the following very approximate guidelines. We emphasize that these are incomplete and that there is significant uncertainty about them, a reflection of the state of the art in economic valuation in these contexts. We expect information to change rapidly as various efforts are made to supplement existing studies. Note also that there are formidable problems in 'transferring' available estimates of economic value from one context to another, and additional problems of extrapolating values from a single area to a grand total relating to all areas. In the latter case, for example, expansion of some uses will lower the prices that can be expected for the produce. Two lessons emerge:

1   If we discover that biodiversity secures benefits of $X in area A we cannot legitimately assume that the same or even similar levels of benefit will apply to area B. This is the transferability problem.

2   If we discover that biodiversity secures benefits of $X in area A we cannot assume that more activity of the same kind will also achieve returns of $X. The act of expanding the activity will alter its price through the forces of supply and demand, and hence will alter its rate of return. This is the extensification problem.

These problems, together with the formidable problems involved in obtaining any monetary estimates in the first place, have to be borne in mind when interpreting the summary data that follow.

Tables 9.1–9.4 summarize some of the results from the overview of biodiversity benefits obtained in Chapter 6. Table 9.1 suggests

Table 9.1 *Ecosystem: tropical forest*
Present values $/hectare (r = 5%, T = 20, sum discount factors = 12.5)

Benefit	Local	Global	Local and Global
Use value: direct			
Medicinal plants	250–750	12–250	262–1000
Tourism	20–1250		20–1250
Minor products	>0–7000		>0–7000
Use value: indirect			
Carbon fixing	0?	1000–4000	1000–4000
Flood control	23		23
Non-use value	+	5	5+
Total*	>293–9023	1017–4255	1310–13278

* the risks in aggregation are discussed in the text

that a tropical forest area could yield anything from $300–$9000 ha in present value terms per ha. This total is heavily influenced by minor forest products and these in turn are seriously affected by the extensification qualification above. Hence we suspect the upper end of this range is in fact unrepresentative.

Table 9.2 shows the results for wetlands. Again, the returns are significant at the local level. Table 9.3 shows the results for rangeland and one wilderness area. Since the wilderness area is for a developed economy (Australia) and was the subject of massive public attention, it would be extremely dangerous to extrapolate the very high per hectare figure implied. For range areas generally the returns appear to be low – of the order of a few dollars per hectare – but this may still be above the opportunity cost of the land if that cost is measured in undistorted economic prices. We have not detailed marine areas separately as so little information is available on them. The Galapagos study discussed in Chapter 6 suggests direct use values of around $600 per hectare (present value) and $65 of indirect use value, but again, the uniqueness of the area needs to be borne in mind. Overall, the results are extremely imperfect but, as a very rough estimate, they suggest that tropical forest area and wetland areas might yield returns of the order of $3000–7000 per hectare in present value terms. Such returns are clearly attractive.

Table 9.2 *Ecosystem: wetlands*
Present values $/ha (r = 5%, T = 20, sum discount factors = 12.5)

Benefit	Local: LDC	Local: DC	Global	Total
Use value: direct				
agriculture + fish + fuel	23			
forestry + fish + recreation	5200–7155		na	na
fur		90		
recreation		27–1624		
water		38,000		
Use value: indirect				
storm protection		1134		
Non-use value		300–350		
Total	23–7155	1600–3200	na	na
		up to 40,000		

Table 9.3 *Ecosystem: rangeland*
Present values $/ha (r = 5%, T = 20, sum discount factors = 12.5)

Benefit	Country	Local Benefit
Use value: direct		
wild products	Zimbabwe	7.5
trophies	Zimbabwe	1.2
viewing	Kenya	<40.0
ranching	Zimbabwe	2.0
Use value: indirect	na	na
Non-use value		
elephants	Thailand	22.0
wilderness	Australia	796,800 to 1,907,600[*]

Note: [*] A$53 to 124 per annum, over 10 years, discounted at 5%, across 12.26m adults and converted to US$ at 1.26$A = $1

The issue is whether such returns are higher than the 'true' opportunity cost of sustainable use of biodiversity and higher than the distorted returns. Table 9.4 summarizes the picture on the opportunity costs of sustainable biodiversity use. The table suggests that sustainable uses could well compete with the true economic alternative such as agriculture and forestry, but that this comparison becomes doubtful when the returns are evaluated in terms of the private gains of the land owner or user. Economic distortions can easily double the private rate of return compared to the economic rate of return, making it more difficult for biodiversity use to compete.

Table 9.4 *Present values of 'development' options*
(r = 5%, T = 20, sum discount factors = 12.5 $/ha)

	Private	National
Forestry	200–500 (sustainable) 1000–2500 (unsustainable)	na
Crops		
General LDC, USA	2700–4630	1660–2320
Japan, NICs	up to 100,000	5800
Livestock	large	negative to small

CONCLUSIONS

Is the sustainable use of biodiversity attractive? The reality is that it all depends on the following factors:

- the location and institutional conditions prevailing. It is not possible to say that sustainable biodiversity use is generally to be preferred to alternative land uses since rates of return will clearly vary according to climate, soil conditions, topography, infrastructure, nearness to market, etc;

- but the limited information available does not support the opposite view. Indeed, it suggests that biodiversity use may well be able to compete with the more traditional land uses if there is greater parity. What this means is that sustainable land use competes with alternative land uses if those uses are not subject to privilege and special fiscal treatment, distorted property rights etc. Where such distortions are present – and they are pervasive – biodiversity use may well fail to 'compete'. Indeed, this is one dominant reason why more investment in biodiversity does not automatically take place;

- this problem is compounded by a second distortion – the absence of 'global markets' in the benefits of biodiversity. In particular, we note that developing countries face major problems of appropriating the global benefits of sustainable use of biodiversity. As long as those global values cannot be captured by host countries, biodiversity will be a risky investment in many contexts. The means of appropriation include resource transfers under conventional aid, transfers under the GEF, debt-for-nature swaps etc. It is imperative that these mechanisms be strengthened and added to. It is also essential that we secure an improved idea of what these global values are in terms of economic quantities;

- despite these cautions, the estimates we have drawn together do suggest that there must be many cases where biodiversity investment 'pays'. Wetlands with the potential for human use, and tropical forests are perhaps the clearest examples, but this conclusion may be influenced by the fact that these systems have been the most studied to date. We suspect that coastal systems would reveal similar high rates of economic return if properly evaluated.

REFERENCES

Abramovitz, J (1991) *Investing in Biodiversity: US Research and Conservation Efforts in Developing Countries* World Resources Institute, Washington DC

Adamowicz, W (1994) *Stated Preference Methods for Environmental Valuation* Paper presented at the Agricultural Economics Society Annual Conference, University of Exeter, April

Adamowicz, W, Asafu-Adajaye, J, Boxall, P C, Phillips, W (1991) 'Components of the Economic Value of Wildlife: An Alberta Study' *The Canadian Field-Naturalist*, vol 105(3), pp 423–429

Adamowicz, W, Phillips, W, Pattison, W (1986) 'The Distribution of Economic Benefits from Alberta Duck Production' *Wildlife Society Bulletin*, vol 14, no 4

Alexandratos, N (ed) (1988) *World Agriculture: Towards 2000* Belhaven Press, London

Antonovic, J (1990) 'Genetically based measures of uniqueness', in Orians, G H, Brown, G M, Kunin, W E, Swierzinbinski, J E (eds) *The Preservation and Valuation of Genetic Resources*, University of Washington Press, Seattle, pp 94–118

Arrow, K et al (1993) 'Report of the NOAA panel on contingent valuations' *US Federal Register*, 15 January, vol 58, no 10, 4602–4614

Asafu-Adjaye, J, Phillips, W, Adamowicz, W (1989) *Towards the Measurement of Total Economic Value: The Case of Wildlife Resources in Alberta* Staff paper no 89-16, Department of Rural Economy, University of Alberta, Edmonton, Alberta

Association of Environmental and Resource Economists Workshop (1992) *Benefits Transfer: Procedures, Problems, and Research Needs* Case Study Synopses

Balick, M, Mendelsohn, R (1992) 'Assessing the Economic Value of Traditional Medicines from Tropical Rainforests' *Conservation Biology*, vol 6, no 1, March

Bann, C (1993) *The Private Sector and Global Warming Mitigation* Centre for Social and Economic Research on the Global Environment, University College London, (*mimeo*)

Barbier, E, Adams, W, Kimmage, K (1991) *Economic Valuation of Wetland Benefits: The Hadejiia-Jama'are Floodplain, Nigeria* London Environmental Economics Centre, Paper 91-02, London

Barbier, E, Burgess, J, Swanson, T, Pearce, D W (1990) *Elephants, Economics and Ivory* Earthscan, London

Barbier, E (1989) *The Economic Value of Ecosystems: 1 Tropical Wetlands* LEEC, Gatekeeper series no 89–02

Barnes, J, Pearce, D W (1991) 'The Mixed Use of Habitat', Centre for Social and Economic Research on the Global Environment, University College London and University of East Anglia (*mimeo*)

Barnes, J (1990) Department of Wildlife and National Parks, Botswana

Barrett, S (1993a) *Joint Implementation for Achieving National Abatement Commitments in the Framework Convention on Climate Change* Report to the Environment Directorate, Organisation for Economic Cooperation and Development (OECD), Paris; London Business School and Centre for Social and Economic Research on the Global Environment, University College London (*mimeo*)

Barrett, S (1993b) *A Strategic Analysis of 'Joint Implementation' Mechanisms in the Framework Convention on Climate Change* Report to the United Nations Conference on Trade and Development (UNCTAD), Geneva. London Business School and Centre for Social and Economic Research on the Global Environment, University College London (*mimeo*)

Bateman, I et al (1992) 'A Contingent Valuation Study of the Norfolk Broads' Report to the National Rivers Authority

Bennett, E, Reynolds, C (1993) 'The value of a mangrove area in Sarawak' in *Biodiversity and Conservation* 2, pp 359–375

Bennett, J (1984) 'Using Direct Questioning to Value the Existence Benefits of Preserve Natural Areas' *Australian Journal of Agricultural Economics* vol 28, nos 2 and 3, August/December, pp 136–152

Benson, J F, Willis, K J (1990) *The Aggregate Value of Non-Priced Recreation Benefits of the Forestry Commission Estate* Report to the Forestry Commission, University of Newcastle Upon Tyne

Bergstrom J, Stoll, J, Titre, J and Wright, V (1990) 'Economic Value of Wetlands-Based Recreation' *Ecological Economics*, vol 2, no 2, June, pp 129–148

Binswanger, H (1989) *Brazilian Policies that Encourage Deforestation in the Amazon* World Bank, Environment Department, Working Paper no 16, Washington DC

Biogeography and Conservation Project, Biodiversity Programme, The Natural History Museum, Cromwell Road, London SW7 5BD

Blamey, R, Common, M (1993) *Stepping Back from Contingent Valuation*

Centre for Resource and Environmental Studies, Australian National University, Canberra

Blum, E (1993) 'Making Biodiversity Conservation Profitable: a Case Study of the Merck INBio Agreement', *Environment*, vol 35, no 4, May

Boado, E (1989) 'Incentive Policies and Forest Use in the Philippines' in Repetto and Gillis (1988)

Boadu, F O (1992) 'Contingent Valuation for Household Water in Rural Ghana' *Journal of Agricultural Economics*, vol 43, no 3

Bohn, A and Byerlee, D (1993) *The Wheat Breeding Industry in Developing Countries: An Analysis of Investments and Impacts* Centro Internacional de CIMMYT, Singapore

Boyd, R and Hyde, W (1989) *Forestry Sector Intervention: the Impacts of Public Regulation on Social Welfare* Iowa State University Press

Boyle, K and Bergstrom, J (1992) 'Benefit Transfer Studies: Myths, Pragmatism, and Idealism' in *Water Resources Research* 28(3), pp 657–663

Bromley, D and Cernea, M (1989) *The Management of Common Property Resources: Some conceptual and operational fallacies* World Bank Discussion Paper no 57

Brookshire, D, David, S, Ives, B, Schulze, W (1976) 'The Valuation of Aesthetic Preferences' *Journal of Environmental Economics and Management* 3, no 3, pp 325–346

Brookshire, D S and Neill, H R (1992) 'Benefit Transfers: Conceptual and Empirical Issues' *Water Resources Research*, vol 28, no 3, March, pp 651–655

Browder, J O (1988a) 'The Social Costs of Rainforest Destruction' *Interciencia*, vol 13, no 2

Browder, J O (1988b) 'Public Policy and Deforestation in the Brazilian Amazon' in Repetto, R and Gillis, M (1988)

Brown, G and Henry, W (1989) *The Economic Value of Elephants* LEEC Paper 89-12, London

Brown, K (1992) *Carbon Sequestration and Storage in Tropical Forests* Centre for Social and Economic Research on the Global Environment, Discussion Paper 92 (forthcoming), University of East Anglia and University College London, Norwich and London

Brown, K and Goldin, I (1992) *The Future of Agriculture: Developing Country Implications* Development Centre Studies, OECD, Paris

Carson, R et al (1992) *A contingent valuation study of lost passive use values resulting from the Exxon Valdez oil spill* Report to the Attorney General of the State of Alaska

Carter, M (1987) *Economic and Socio-economic Impacts of the Thorns Starfish on the Great Barrier Reef* Report to the Great Barrier Reef Marine Park Authority, Institute of Applied Environmental Research, Griffith University, Brisbane

Cervigni, R (1993a) *Biodiversity, Incentives to Deforest and Tradeable Development Rights* GEC Working Paper 93-07, Centre for Social and Economic Research on the Global Environment, University of East Anglia, University College London

Cervigni, R (1993b) *Estimating the benefits of plant genetic resources for food and agriculture: Suggested Approaches* Centre for Social and Economic Research on the Global Environment, University College London and University of East Anglia (*mimeo*)

Cesario, F J (1976) 'Value of Time in Recreation Benefit Studies' *Land Economics*, vol 52, pp 32–41

Child, B (1990a) 'Assessment of Wildlife Utilization as a Land Use Option in the Semi-Arid Rangelands of Southern Africa' in Kiss, A (ed) *Living with Wildlife. Wildlife Resource Management with Local Participation in Africa* World Bank, Washington DC, pp 155–176

Child, B (1990b) 'Economic Analysis of Buffalo Range Ranch' in Kiss, A (ed) *Living with Wildlife Resource Management with Local Participation in Africa* World Bank, Washington DC, Annex 3, pp 193–204

Child, G (1984) 'Managing Wildlife for People in Zimbabwe' in McNeely, J and Miller, K (eds) *National Parks, Conservation and Development* Smithsonian Institute, Washington DC

Cichetti, C, Fisher, A, Smith, V K (1971) 'An Econometric Evaluation of a Generalized Consumer Surplus Measure: The Mineral King Controversy' in *Econometrica* 39, pp 813–827

Cline, W (1992) *The Economics of Global Warming* International Institute for International Economics, Washington DC

Common, M S (1973) 'A Note on the Use of the Clawson Method for the Evaluation of Recreational Sight Benefits' *Regional Studies*, vol 7, pp 401–406

Cooper, D, Vellvé, R and Hobbelink, H (eds) (1992) *Growing Diversity: Genetic Resources and Local Food Security* London: Intermediate Technology Publications

Costanza, R, Farber, S and Maxwell, J (1989) 'Valuation and Management of Wetland Ecosystems' *Ecological Economics*, vol 1, no 4, December, pp 335–362

Coulson, I M (1990) *Tsetse Fly Eradication in Matusadona National Park. Integrated Environmental Planning to Reduce Conflicts with Conservation and Tourism* Dept of National Parks and Wildlife Management, Harare

Coyne, A G and Adamowicz, W L (1992) 'Modelling Choice of Site for Hunting Bighorn Sheep' *Wildlife Society Bulletin* 20, pp 26–33

Cummings, R G, Brookshire, D S and Schulze, W D (1986) *Valuing Environmental Goods: An Assessment of the Contingent Valuation Method* Rowman & Allanheld, Totowa, NJ

Danielson, L E, Leitch, J A (1986) 'Private Versus Public Economics of

Prairie Wetland Allocation' *Journal of Environmental Economics and Management* vol 13, no 1, March

Deacon, R and Murphy, P (1992) *The Structure of an Environmental Transaction: the Debt-for-Nature Swap* Department of Economics, University of California at Santa Barbara (*mimeo*)

de Groot, R (1992) *Functions and Values of Protected Areas: A Comprehensive Framework for Assessing the Benefits of Protected Areas to Human Society* Climate Change Research Centre, Agricultural University, Wageningen, Netherlands

DeLacy, T and Lockwood, M *Estimating the Non-Market Values of Nature Conservation Resources Australia* Charles Sturt University, Albury, Australia

Dept of National Parks and Wildlife Management (1991) *Annual Report of the Warden (Tourism)*, Dept of National Parks and Wildlife Management, Harare

Desvousges, W H, Gable, A R, Dunford, R W, Hudson, S (1993) 'Contingent Valuation: the wrong tool to measure passive-use losses' *Choices*, second quarter, pp 9–11

Dinerstein, E and Wikramanayake, E (1993) 'Beyond Hotspots: How to prioritise Investments to Conserve Biodiversity in the Indo-Pacific Region' *Conservation Biology*, 7(1), pp 53–65

Dixon, J A, Scura, L F, van't Hof, T (1993) 'Meeting Ecological and Economic Goals: Marine Parks in the Caribbean' in *Ambio* 22(2–3), pp 117–125

Dixon, J A and Sherman, P B (1990) *Economics of Protected Areas, A New Look at the Benefits and Costs* Earthscan, London

Dixon, R et al (1993) 'Forest Sector Carbon Offset Projects: Near-Term Opportunities to Mitigate Greenhouse Gas Emissions' *Water, Air and Soil Pollution*, special issue.

Dobias, R J (1988) *Influencing Decision Makers About Providing Enhanced Support For Protected Areas in Thailand (Beneficial Use Project)* WWF Contract 3757 Interim Report, Bangkok: WWF Thailand (*mimeo*)

Dogse, P and von Droste, B (1990) *Debt for Nature Exchanges and Biosphere Reserves* UNESCO, Paris

Ehrlich, P R and A H (1992) 'The Value of Biodiversity' *Ambio*, vol 21 no 3

Evenson, R E (1991) 'Genetic resources: assessing economic value' in Vincent, J, Crawford, E, Hoehn, J (ed) *Valuing Environmental Benefits in Developing Economies* Proceedings of a seminar series held February–May 1990 at Michigan State University, Special Report no 29

Faeth, P, Cort, C, Livernash, R (1994) *Evaluating the Carbon Sequestration Benefits of Forestry Projects in Less Developed Countries* World Resources Institute, Washington DC

Faith, D P (1994) 'Genetic Diversity and Taxonomic Priorities for Conservation' *Biological Conservation*, pp 68, 69–74

Fankhauser, S (1992) *A Point Estimate of the Economic Damage from Global Warming* Centre for Social and Economic Research on the Global Environment, CSERGE Discussion Paper 92, University of East Anglia and University College London, Norwich and London

Fankhauser, S (1994) 'The Social Costs of Greenhouse Gas Emissions: An Expected Value Approach' in *The Energy Journal*, 15 (2), forthcoming

Farber, S and Costanza, R (1987) 'The Value of Coastal Wetlands for Protection of Property against Hurricane Wind Damage' *Journal of Environmental Economics and Management*, 14, 143–151

Farnsworth, N (1986) 'Screening Plants for New Medicines' in Wilson, E O (ed) *Biodiversity* National Academy, Washington DC

Findeisen, C (1991) *Natural Products Research and the Potential Role of the Pharmaceutical Industry in Tropical Forest Conservation* Rainforest Alliance, New York (*mimeo*)

Fiselier, J L (1990a) *Living off the Tides* Environmental Database on Wetlands Interventions, Leiden, Netherlands

Fiselier, J L (1990b) *Living off the Flood plains* Environmental Database on Wetlands Interventions, Leiden, Netherlands

Fishbein, M and Azjen, A (1975) *Belief, Attitude, Intention and Behaviour: An Introduction to Theory and Research* Addison-Wesley, Reading, Mass

Freeman, A M III (1979) *The Benefits of Environmental Improvement: Theory and Practice* Johns Hopkins University Press, Baltimore

Furtado, J (1990) *Biological Diversity: Global Conservation Needs and Costs* Environment Programme Report, Centre for Integrated Development, London, UK

Gámez, R et al (1993) 'Costa Rica's Conservation Program and National Biodiversity Institute (INBio)' in Reid, W et al (1993) *Biodiversity Prospecting: Using Genetic Resources for Sustainable Development* World Resources Institute, Washington DC

Gillis, M (1988a) 'Indonesia: Public Policies, Resource Management and the Tropical Forest' in Repetto, R and Gillis, M (1988)

Gillis, M (1988b) 'Malaysia: Public Policies and the Tropical Forest' in Repetto and Gillis (1988)

Gillis, M (1988c) 'West Africa: Resource Management Policies and the Tropical Forest' in Repetto and Gillis (1988)

Global Environment Facility (1992) *Memorandum of Understanding on Norwegian Funding of Pilot Demonstration Projects for Joint Implementation Arrangements Under the Climate Convention* GEF, World Bank, Washington DC (*mimeo*)

Godoy, R and Bawa, K (1993) 'The Economic Value and Sustainable

Harvest of Plants and Animals from the Tropical Rainforest: Assumptions, Hypotheses, and Methods' in *Economic Botany*, 47 (3), pp 215–219

Godoy, R, Lubowski, R, Markandya, A (1993) 'A Method for the Economic Valuation of Non-timber Tropical Forest Products' in *Economic Botany*, 47 (3), pp 220–233

Goldwin, I (1990) *Comparative Advantage: Theory and Application to Developing Country Agriculture* Technical Paper 16, OECD Development Centre, OECD, Paris

Goodland, R and Webb, M (1987) *The Management of Cultural Property in World Bank Assisted Projects* World Bank Technical Paper 62

Gradwohl, J and Greenberg, R (1988) *Saving the Tropical Forests* Earthscan, London

Grimes, A et al (1993) 'Valuing the rainforest: The economic value of non-timber forest products in Ecuador', Yale School of Forestry and Environmental Studies, New Haven (*mimeo*)

Gutierrez, B, Pearce, D W (1992) *Estimating the Environmental Benefits of the Amazon Forest: an Intertemporal Valuation Exercise* GEC Working Paper 92-44, Centre for Social and Economic Research on the Global Environment, University College London and University of East Anglia

Hall, P and Bawa, K (1993) 'Methods to Assess the Impact of Extraction of Non-timber Tropical Forest Products on Plant Populations' in *Economic Botany*, 47 (3), pp 234–247

Hamilton, L, Snedaker, S (eds) (1984) *Handbook for Mangrove Area Management* UNEP and East West Centre, Hawaii

Hanemann, W M (1989) 'Welfare Evaluations in Contingent Valuation: Experiments with Discrete Responses' in *American Journal of Agricultural Economics* 66 (3), pp 32–341

Hanemann, W M (1989) 'Welfare Evaluations in Contingent Valuation: Experiments with Discrete Response Data: Reply' in *American Journal of Agricultural Economics*

Hanemann, W M (1991) 'Willingness to Pay and Willingness to Accept: How Much Can They Differ?' *American Economic Review*, vol 81, no 3, June, pp 633–647

Hanley, N and Craig, S (1991) 'Wilderness development decisions and the Krutilla-Fisher model: the case of Scotland's Flow country' *Ecological Economics*, 4 (2), pp 145–162

Hanley, N D (1990) 'Valuation of Environmental Effects: Final Report – Stage One', Industry Department of Scotland and the Scottish Development Agency

Hanley, N and Spash, C (1993) *Preferences, Information and Biodiversity Preservation* Discussion Papers in Economics 93/12, Department of Economics, University of Stirling

Hardin, G (1968) 'The Tragedy of the Commons' *Science* vol 162, no 6, pp 368–373

Harmon, D (1992) *Indicators of the World's Cultural Diversity* The George Wright Society, Michigan, USA

Hausman, J A, Leonard, G K, McFadden, D (1992) *Assessing Use Value Losses Due to Natural Resource Injury* Cambridge Economics Inc., Cambridge, Massachusetts

Heath, R (1992a) *Wildlife Based Tourism in a Developing Country: The Economic Implications* University of Zimbabwe

Heath, R (1992b) *The Growth in Wildlife Based Tourism in Zimbabwe* University of Zimbabwe

Heberlein, T A (1986) 'Measuring Resource Values: The Reliability and Validity of Dichotomous Contingent Valuation Measures', Paper presented at the American Sociological Association Meeting, New York, August

Hecht, S, Norgaard, R and Possio, G (1988) 'The Economics of Cattle Ranching in Eastern Amazonia' *Interciencia*, vol 13, no 5, Sept–Oct, pp 233–239

Hof, J and King, D (1991) 'Recreational Demand by Tourists for Saltwater Beach Days: Comment' *Journal of Environmental Economics and Management*, 22, pp 281–291

Hohl, A and Tisdell, C (1993) 'How useful are environmental safety standards in economics? – The example of safe minimum standards for protection of species' *Biodiversity and Conservation*, 2, pp 168–181

Holdgate, M et al (1982) *The World Environment 1972–1982* United Nations Environment Programme, Nairobi

Huber, R (1992) 'Case Studies Showing Cost/Benefit of Tourism and Protected Areas Development', Paper presented at The IV World Congress on National Parks and Protected Areas, Caracas 10–21 February

Hundloe, T J (1990) 'Measuring the Value of the Great Barrier Reef' *Australian Parks and Recreation* 26 (3), pp 11–15

Imber, D, Stevenson, G, Wilks, L (1991) *A Contingent Valuation Survey of the Kakadu Conservation Zone* Resource Assessment Commission, Research Paper no 3, Canberra, February

IUCN (1991) 'Protected Areas of the World: A Review of National Systems' *Afrotropical*, vol 3

IUCN (1992) *Regional Reviews* IVth World Congress on National Parks and Protected Areas, Caracas, Venezuela, 10–21 February 1992

Jansen, D J (1990) *Sustainable Wildlife Utilization in the Zambezi Valley of Zimbabwe: economic, ecological and political tradeoffs* Project Paper no 10, WWF Multispecies Project, Harare

Johansson, P, Kristrom, B, Maler, K (1989) 'Welfare Evaluations in

Contingent Valuation: Experiments with Discrete Response Data: Comment' in *American Journal of Agricultural Economics*

Kahneman, D, Knetsch, J L and Thaler, R H (1990) 'Experimental Tests of the Endowment Effect and the Coase Theorem' *Journal of Political Economy* vol 98, no 6

Kahneman, D and Knetsch, J (1992) 'Valuing Public Goods: The Purchase of Moral Satisfaction' *Journal of Environmental Economics and Management* vol 22, no 1, pp 57–70

Kahneman, D and Tversky, A (1979) 'Prospect Theory: An Analysis of Decisions Under Risk' *Econometrica*, vol 47, no 2, pp 263–291

Katzman, M and Cale, W (1990) 'Tropical Forest Preservation Using Economic Incentives: A proposal of conservation easements' *BioScience*, 40 (11), pp 827–832

Klepper, S, Leamer, E (1984) 'Consistent sets of estimates for restricted regressions with errors in all variables' *Econometrica*, 52 (1), pp 163–183

Kling, C L (1987) 'A Simulation Approach to Comparing Multiple-Site Recreation-Demand Models Using Chesapeake Bay Survey Data' *Marine Resource Economics*, vol 4, no 2, pp 95–109

Kling, C L (1988) 'Comparing Welfare Estimates of Environmental Quality Changes from Recreational Demand Models' *Journal of Environmental Economics and Management*, vol 15, no 3, pp 331–340

Knetsch, J (1989) 'The Endowment Effects Evidence of Non-reversible Indifference Curves' *American Economic Review*, vol 79, no 5, pp 1277–1288

Knetsch, J and Sinden, J (1984) 'Willingness to Pay and Compensation Demanded: Experimental Evidence of an Unexpected Disparity in Measures of Value' *Quarterly Journal of Economics*, vol XCIX, no 3, pp 507–521

Kosmo, M (1989) 'Commercial Energy Subsidies in Developing Countries' *Energy Policy* no 17, pp 244–53

Kramer, R, et al (1993) *Valuing a Protected Tropical Forest: A Case Study of Madagascar* Paper prepared for the IVth World Congress of National Parks and Protected Areas, Caracas, Venezuela. February 1992, Centre for Resource and Environmental Policy Research, Duke University, Durham, NC

Krutilla, J and Fisher, A (1985) *The Economics of Natural Environments* Resources for the Future, Washington DC

Laird, S (1993) 'Contracts for Biodiversity Prospecting' in Reid, W et al (1993) *Biodiversity Prospecting: Using Genetic Resources for Sustainable Development* World Resources Institute, Washington DC

Leslie, A J (1987) 'A Second Look at the Economics of Natural Management Systems in Tropical Mixed Forests' *Unasylva*, 39, no 155, pp 46–58

Loehman, E T and V H De (1992) 'Application of Stochastic Choice Modelling to Policy Analysis of Public Goods: A Case Study of Air Quality Improvements' *Review of Economics and Statistics*, 64, pp 474–480

Loomis, J B (1988) 'Contingent Valuation Using Dichotomous Choice Models' in *Journal of Leisure Research* 20 (1), pp 46–56

Loomis, J B (1989) 'Test–Retest Reliability of the Contingent Valuation Method: A Comparison of General Population and Visitor Response' *American Journal of Agricultural Economics* vol 71, pp 76–84

Loomis, J B (1990) 'Comparative Reliability of the Dichotomous Choice And Open Ended Valuation Techniques' *Journal of Environmental Economics and Management* vol 18, no 1, pp 78–85

Louviere, J J (1994) *Relating stated preference measures and models to choices in real markets* Paper prepared for the US Department of Energy and Environmental Protection Agency workshop 'Using contingent valuation to measure non-market values', Herndon, VA, May

Magrath, W and Arens, P (1989) *The Cost of Soil Erosion on Java: A Natural Resource Accounting Approach* Environment Department, Working Paper Number 18, World Bank, Washington DC

Mahar, D (1989) *Government Policies and Deforestation in Brazil's Amazon Region* World Bank, Washington DC

Maille, P, Mendelsohn, R (1993) 'Valuing Ecotourism in Madagascar' in *Journal of Environmental Management* 38, pp 213–218

Mäler, K-G (1977) 'A Note on the Use of Property Values in Estimating Marginal Willingness to Pay for Environmental Quality' *Journal of Environmental Economics and Management* vol 4, no 4, pp 355–369

Marcondes, M (1981) *Adaptation de una metodologia de evaluacion economica, aplicada al Parque Nacional Cahuita, Costa Rica* Centro Agronomico Tropical de Investigacion y Ensenanza (CATIE), Serie Tecnica no 9

Markandya, A and Pearce, D W (1988) *Environmental Considerations and the Choice of the Discount Rate in Developing Countries* World Bank, Environmental Dept Working Paper No 3

McClenagham, L R Jr, Berger, J and Truesdale, H D (1990) 'Founding Lineages and Genetic Variability in Plains Bison (*Bison bison*) from Badlands National Park, South Dakota' *Conservation Biology* 4 (3), pp 285–289

McConnell, K E and Strand, I E (1981) 'Measuring the Cost of Time in Recreation Demand Analysis', *American Journal of Agricultural Economics*, vol 63, pp 153–156

McNeely, J and Tobias, R (1991) 'Economic Incentives For Conserving Biological Diversity in Thailand' *Ambio*, vol 20, no 2, pp 86–90

McNeely, J and Norgaard, R (1991) 'Developed Country Policies and

Biological Diversity in Developing Countries' *Agriculture, Ecosystems and Environment* no 42, pp 194–204

Mendelsohn, R, Hof, J, Petersen, G and Reed, J (1992) 'Measuring Recreation Values with Multiple Destination Trips' *American Journal of Agricultural Economics* 74 (4), pp 926–933

Mendelsohn, R O and Tobias, R (1991) 'Valuing Ecotourism in a Tropical Rainforest Reserve' *Ambio*, vol 20, no 2, pp 91–93

Mercer, E, Kramer, R, Sharma, N (1993) *Estimating the Nature Tourism Benefits of Establishing the Mantadia National Park in Madagascar* Centre for Resource and Environmental Policy Research, Duke University, NC

Milner-Gulland, E J and Leader-Williams, N (1992) 'A Model of Incentives for Illegal Exploitation of Rhinos and Elephants: Poaching Pays in Luangwa Valley, Zambia' *Journal of Applied Ecology*, 29

Ministry of Natural Resources, Energy and Mines, Costa Rica (1991) *National Study of Biodiversity: Costs, Benefits and Needs for Financing and Conservation of Biological Diversity in Costa Rica*

Mitchel, C (1989) *Economics and the Environment: A Case of Small Island States* Prepared for the Caribbean Conservation Association Conference on Economics of the Environment, Barbados

Montgomery, C, Brown, G M, Adams, D (1994) 'The Marginal Cost of Species Preservation: The Northern Spotted Owl' *Journal of Environmental Economics and Management* 26 (2) pp 111–128

Mooney, P R (1993) 'Exploiting Local Knowledge: international policy implications' in de Boef Amanor, W, Wellard, K, Bebbington, A (ed) *Cultivating Knowledge: Genetic diversity, farmer experimentation and crop research* Intermediate Technology Publications, London

Moran, D (1994) 'Contingent valuation and biodiversity conservation in Kenyan protected areas' *Biodiversity and Conservation* (forthcoming)

Morey, E R, Shaw, W D and Rowe, R D (1991) 'A Discrete-Choice Model of Recreational Participation, Site Choice, and the Activity Valuation When Complete Trip Data are not Available' *Journal of Environmental Economics and Management*, vol 20, pp 181–201

Munasinghe, M (1992) *Economic and Policy Issues in Natural Habitat and Protected Areas* World Bank, Washington DC

Myers, N (1991a) 'Biological Diversity and Global Security' in Bormann, F H and Kellert, S R (eds) *Ecology, Economics, Ethics: The Broken Circle* Yale University Press

Myers, N (1991b) 'Tropical Forests: Present Status and Future Outlook' *Climatic Change*, 19, pp 3–32

Myers, N (ed) (1991c) 'Tropical Forests and Climate' *Climatic Change*, 19, pp 1–2

Myers, N (1993) 'Questions of mass extinction' *Biodiversity and Conservation*, 2, pp 2–17

Newcombe, K and de Lucia, R (1993) *Mobilising Private Capital Against Global Warming: a Business Concept and Policy Issues* Global Environmental Facility, Washington DC (*mimeo*)

NOAA (National Oceanic and Atmospheric Administration) (1994) Oil Pollution Act of 1990: Proposed Regulations for Natural Resource Damage Assessments, US Department of Commerce

Nordhaus, W (1991a) 'To Slow or Not To Slow: The Economics of the Greenhouse Effect' *Economic Journal*, vol 101, no 6, pp. 920–937

Nordhaus, W (1991b) 'A Sketch of Economics of the Greenhouse Effect' *American Economic Review*, vol 81, no 2, May, pp 146–150

Norton, B G and Ulanowocz, R E (1992) 'Scale and Biodiversity Policy: A Hierarchical Approach' *Ambio*, 21 (3), pp 244–249

Norton-Griffiths, M, Southey, C (1994) 'The opportunity costs of biodiversity conservation: a case study of Kenya' *Ecological Economics* (forthcoming)

Noss, R F, Cline, S, Csuti, B, Scott, M (1992) 'Monitoring and assessing biodiversity' in Lykke, E (ed) *Achieving Environmental Goals: The Concept and Practice of Environmental Performance Review*, Belhaven Press, London

O'Connor, S and Langrand, O (1992) *Can Wildlife Pay Its Way in Madagascar?* World Wildlife Fund for Nature, Madagascar

OECD (Organisation for Economic Cooperation and Development) (1992) *Development Cooperation: 1992 Report* OECD, Paris

OECD (1993) *Agricultural Policies, Markets and Trade: Monitoring and Outlook 1993*, OECD, Paris

Padoch, C, de Jong, W (1989) 'Production and profit in agroforestry: an example from the Peruvian Amazon' in Browder, J G (ed) *Fragile Lands of Latin America: strategies for sustainable development* Westview Press, Boulder, CO

Panayoutou, T (1994) 'Conservation of Biodiversity and Economic Development: The Concept of Transferable Development Right' in Perrings, C et al *Biodiversity Conservation: Policy Issues and Options* Amsterdam: Kluwer Academic Press (forthcoming)

Pearce, D W (1986) *Cost-Benefit Analysis* Macmillan, Basingstoke

Pearce, D W (1990) *An Economic Approach to Saving the Tropical Forests* LEEC Paper 90-06, London

Pearce, D W (1991a) *Economic Valuation and the Natural World* Earthscan Publications, London

Pearce, D W (ed) (1991b) *Blueprint 2: Greening the World Economy* Earthscan Publications, London

Pearce, D W (1991c) *Economic Valuation and the Natural World* Centre for Social and Economic Research on the Global Environment, University College London and University of East Anglia

Pearce, D W (1991d) 'Deforesting the Amazon: Toward an Economic Solution' *Ecodecision*, 1, pp 40–49

Pearce, D W (1992a) 'Discounting' in Pearce, D W, Whittington, James, D and Georgiou, S *Manual of Environmental Projects and Policy Appraisal* OECD, Paris

Pearce, D W (1992b) *Assessing the Social Rate of Return in Temperate Zone Forestry* Centre for Social and Economic Research on the Global Environment, University College London and University of East Anglia (*mimeo*)

Pearce, D W (1994) *Capturing Global Environmental Values* Centre for Social and Economic Research on the Global Environment University College London and University of East Anglia (*mimeo*)

Pearce, D W et al (1993) *Mexico Forestry and Conservation Sector Review: substudy of economic valuation of forests* Report to Latin American Technical Department, World Bank, Washington DC

Pearce, D W, Bann, C and Georgiou, S (1992) *The Social Costs of Fuel Cycles* Centre for Social and Economic Research on the Global Environment, University College London (*mimeo*)

Pearce, D W and Barbier, E (1987) *Forest Policy in Indonesia* World Bank, Washington DC (*mimeo*)

Pearce, D W, Barbier, E and Markandya, A (1990) *Sustainable Development* Edward Elgar, London and (1991) Earthscan, London

Pearce, D W and Warford, J (1992) *World Without End: Economics, Environment and Sustainable Development* Oxford University Press, Oxford and New York

Pechmann, J H K et al (1991) 'Declining Amphibian Populations: The Problem of Separating Human Impacts from Natural Fluctuations' *Science*, 253, pp 892–895

Perrings, C, Pearce, D W (1994) 'Threshold Effects and Incentives for the Conservation of Biodiversity' *Environmental and Resource Economics*, 4, pp 13–28

Peters, C M, Gentry, A H, Mendelsohn, R O (1989) 'Valuation of an Amazonian Rainforest' *Nature*, vol 339, June 29, pp 655–656

Phillips, W E, Adamowicz, W L, Asafu-Adjaye, J and Boxall, P C (1989) *An Economic Assessment of the Wildlife Resource in Alberta* Project Report no 89-04, Alberta Recreation, Parks and Wildlife Foundation

Pinedo-Vasquez, M, Zarin, D, Jipp, P (1992) 'Economic returns from forest conversion in the Peruvian Amazon' *Ecological Economics*, vol 6, pp 163–173

Posner, B et al (1981) 'Economic Impact Analysis for the Virgin Island Resources Foundation' St Thomas, US Virgin Islands

Principe, P (1989) 'The Economic Significance of Plants and their Constituents as Drugs' in Wagner, H, Hikino, H and Farnsworth, N *Eco-*

nomic and Medicinal Plant Research, Academic Press, London, vol 3, pp 1–17

Principe, P (1991) 'Monetizing the Pharmacological Benefits of Plants' US Environmental Protection Agency, Washington DC (*mimeo*)

Randall, A, Stoll, J (1983) 'Existence Values in a Total Valuation Framework' in Row, R D and Chestnut, L G *Managing Air Quality and Scenic Resources at National Parks and Wilderness Areas* Westview Press, Boulder, Colorado

Raven, P (1988) 'Our Diminishing Tropical Forests' in Wilson, E O (ed) *Biodiversity*, Washington DC

Reid, W et al (1992) *Developing Indicators of Biodiversity Conservation* World Resources Institute Draft Report, Washington

Reid, W et al (1993) *Biodiversity Prospecting: Using Genetic Resources for Sustainable Development* World Resources Institute, Washington DC

Reid, W et al (1993) 'A New Lease of Life' in Reid, W et al (1993) *Biodiversity Prospecting: Using Genetic Resources for Sustainable Development* World Resources Institute, Washington DC

Reid, W V and Miller, K R (1989) *Keeping Options Alive: The Scientific Basis for Conserving Biodiversity* World Resources Institute, Washington DC

Repetto, R (1986) *World Enough and Time* Yale University Press, New Haven

Repetto, R (1988) *The Forest for the Trees? Government Policies and the Misuse of Forest Resources* World Resource Institute, Washington DC

Repetto, R and Gillis, M (eds) (1988) *Public Policies and the Misuse of Forest Resources* Cambridge University Press, Cambridge

Repetto (1985) see Pearce and Warford chap

Rosenthal, D, Nelson R (1992) 'Why Existence Value Should Not be Used in Cost-Benefit Analysis' *Journal of Policy Analysis and Management* 11 (1) pp 116–122

Ruitenbeek, H J (1989a) *Social Cost Benefit Analysis of the Korup Project, Cameroon* WWF Report prepared for the World Wide Fund for Nature and the Republic of Cameroon, London, UK

Ruitenbeek, H J (1989b) *Republic of Cameroon: the Korup Project* Cameroon Ministry of Planning and Regional Development, Cameroon

Ruitenbeek, H J (1990a) *Economic Analysis of Tropical Forest Conservation Initiatives: Examples from West Africa* WWF, UK

Ruitenbeek, H J (1990b) 'Evaluating Economic Policies for Promoting Rainforest Conservation in Developing Countries', PhD thesis, London School of Economics and Political Science

Ruitenbeek, H J (1990c) *The Rainforest Supply Price: A Step Towards Estimating a Cost Curve for Rainforest Conservation* The Development Economics Research Programme, London School of Economics

Ruitenbeek, H J (1991) *Mangrove Management: An Economic Analysis of Management Options with a Focus on Bintuni Bay, Irian Jaya*, Ministry of State for Population and Environment, Jakarta

Ruitenbeek, H J (1992) 'The Rainforest Supply Price: A Tool for Evaluating Rainforest Conservation Expenditures' *Ecological Economics*, vol 6, no 1, July, pp 57–78

Sale, J (1991) *Priorities for Support for Protected Area Systems in Developing Countries* IVth World Congress on National Parks and Protected Areas, Caracas, Venezuela

Samples, K, Dixon, J and Gowen, M (1986a) 'Information Disclosure and Endangered Species Valuation' *Land Economics*, vol 62, no 3

Samples, K, Gowen, M and Dixon J (1986b) *The Validity of the Contingent Valuation Method for Estimating Non-Use Components of Preservation Values for Unique Natural Resources* Paper presented to the American Agricultural Economics Association, Reno, July

Schkade, D, Payne, J W (1994) 'How People Respond to Contingent Valuation Questions: A Verbal Protocol Analysis of Willingness to Pay for an Environmental Regulation' in *Journal of Environmental Economics and Management* 26, pp 88–109

Schneider, R (1991) *An Analysis of Environmental Problems and Policies in the Amazon* in Tratado de Cooperacion Amazonica. Seminario Sobre Politicas y Practicas Para Desarrollo Sostenible en los Paises Miembros del Tratado de Cooperacion Amazonica, Informe Final, Caracas

Schneider, R (1992) Brazil: An Analysis of Environmental Problems in the Amazon, Report no 9104-BR, Latin America and Caribbean Region, World Bank, Washington DC

Schramm, G and Warford, J (eds) (1989) *Environmental Management and Economic Development* A World Bank Publication, Washington DC

Schulze, W, d'Arge, R and Brookshire, D (1981) 'Valuing Environmental Commodities: Some Recent Experiments' *Land Economics*, vol 57, no 2

Schulze, W et al (1983) 'Economic Benefits of Preserving Visibility on the National Parklands of the Southwest' *Natural Resources Journal*, 23

Sedjo, R (1987) *The Economics of Natural and Plantation Forests in Indonesia* Resources for the Future, Washington DC (*mimeo*)

Shyamsundar, P, Kramer, R (1993) *Does Contingent Valuation Work in Non-market Economies?* Centre for Resource and Environmental Policy Research, Duke University, Durham, NC

Sittenfield, A and Gámez, R (1993) 'Biodiversity Prospecting in INBio' in Reid et al (1993a)

Smith, V K (1987) 'Non-use Values in Benefit-Cost Analysis' *Southern Economic Journal* 54, pp 19–26

Smith, V K and Desvousges, W H (1986) *Measuring Water Quality Benefits* Kluwer-Nijhoff Publishing, Boston, 54, pp 19–26

Smith, V K and Kaoru, Y (1990) 'Signals or Noise? Explaining the Variation in Recreation Benefit Estimates' *American Journal of Agricultural Economics*, vol 72, pp 419–433

Solorzano, R and Guerrero (1988) Justificacion Economica de la Permanencia del Bosque en Terrenos Forestales de la Reserva Forestal Rio Macho, Costa Rica

Solow (1974) 'The Economics of Resources or the Resources of Economics' *American Economic Review* 64

Stevens, T H, Echeverria, J, Glass, R J, Hager, T, More, T A (1991) 'Measuring Existence Value of Wildlife: What do CVM estimates really show?' *Land Economics*, 67, (4), pp 390–400

Swanson, T (1991) *The Economics of Natural Habitat Utilisation: a Survey of the Literature and Issues* London Environmental Economics Centre, London (*mimeo*)

Swanson, T and Barbier, E (1992) *Economics for the Wilds: Wildlife, Wildlands, Diversity and Development* Earthscan, London

Thibodeau, F and Ostro, B (1981) 'An Economic Analysis of Wetland Protection' *Journal of Environmental Management* vol 12, no 1, January

Thomas, D H L, Ayache, F and Hollis, T (1990) 'Use Values and Non-Use Values in the Conservation of Ichkeul National Park, Tunisia' *Environmental Conservation 18, 2, pp 119–130*

Tickell, O (1992) 'Nuts, Bucks and Survival' *Geographical Magazine*, August, pp 10–14

Tisdell, C (1992) *Environmental Economic Guidelines – Inter-country and Inter-regional requests for Financial Support for Protected Areas: What Factors, Especially Economic Factors, might be Important in Ranking These* University of Queensland, Brisbane, Australia

Tobias, R and Mendelsohn, R (1991) 'Valuing Ecotourism in a Tropical Rainforest Reserve' *Ambio*, vol 20, no 2, pp 91–93

Turner, K, Brooke, J (1988) 'Management and Valuation of an Environmentally Sensitive Area: Norfolk Broadland Case Study' *Environmental Management*, vol 12, no 3

Turner, K and Jones, T (ed) (1991) *Wetlands: Market and Intervention Failures; Four Case Studies*, Earthscan, London

UNEP (1992a) Biodiversity Country Studies, Synthesis Report

UNEP (1992b) Uganda: Country Study on Costs, Benefits, and Unmet Needs of Biological Diversity Conservation

UNEP (1992c) Bahamas: Country Study on Biodiversity; Census, Analysis, Conservation Costs, Benefits and Unmet Needs

UNEP (1992d) Indonesian Country Study on Biological Diversity

UNEP (1992e) Country Study Report for Nigerian Costs, Benefits and Unmet Needs of Biological Diversity Conservation

UNEP-Annex (1991) Biodiversity in Thailand: Research Priorities for Sustainable Development

van Diepen, P, Fiselier, J (1990) 'The Bintuni Case: Nature Under Siege' in Marchand, M and Udo de Haes, H A (eds) *Proceedings of the International Conference on Wetlands: The People's Role in Wetland Management* Leiden, 5–8 June 1989, Centre for Environmental Studies, Leiden

Vincent, J (1990) 'Rent Capture and the Feasibility of Tropical Forest Management' *Land Economics*, vol 66, no 2, May, pp 212–223

Vitousek, P et al (1986) 'Human Appropriation of Products of Photosynthesis' *Bioscience*, vol 36, no 6, pp 368–373

Walsh, R G, Johnson, D M, McKean, J R (1992) 'Benefit Transfer of Outdoor Recreation Demand Studies, 1968–1988' *Water Resources Research*, vol 28, no 3, March, (Special Section: Problems and Issues in the Validity of Benefit Transfer Methodologies)

Walsh, R, Rosenthal, R D (1990) 'Estimating the Public Benefits of Protecting Forest Quality' *Journal of Environmental Management*, 30, pp 175–189

Warren, D M (1991) *Using Indigenous Knowledge in Agricultural Development* World Bank Discussion Papers no 127

Watson, D (1988) 'The Evolution of Appropriate Resource Management Systems' in Berkes, F (ed) (1988) *Common Property Resources: Ecology and Community Based Sustainable Development* Belhaven, London

WCMC (World Conservation and Monitoring Centre) (1992) *Global Biodiversity: Status of the Earth's Living Resources* Chapman and Hall, London

Weaver, S M (1991) 'The Role of Aboriginals in the Management of Australia's Coburg (Gurig) and Kakadu National Parks' in West, P C and Brechin, S R (eds) *Resident Peoples and National Parks: Social Dilemmas and Strategies in International Conservation* University of Arizona Press, Tucson, pp 311–333

Webb, A, Lopez, M and Penn, R (1990) *Estimates of Producer and Consumer Subsidy Equivalents: Government Intervention in Agriculture 1982–1987* US Department of Agriculture Statistical Bulletin 803, Washington DC

Wells, M (1992a) 'Fiduciary Funds To Preserve Biodiversity: Green Funds' *Ecologica*, February

Wells, M (1992b) *A Summary of the Benefits, Costs and Risks of Using Environmental Trust Funds for Biodiversity Conservation* Environmental Policy and Research Division, World Bank

Wells, M (1992c) 'Biodiversity Conservation, Affluence and Poverty: Mismatched Costs and Benefits and Efforts to Remedy them' in *Ambio*, 21 (3), pp 237–243

Wendelaar, A, Pearce, D W, Moran, D (1994) *Determining biodiversity conservation priorities* Centre for Social and Economic Research on the Global Environment, University College London, University of East Anglia (forthcoming)

Weston, D and Thresher, P (1973) *Development Plans for Amboseli* World Bank Office, Nairobi

Whittington, D et al (1991) 'Willingness To Pay for Improved Sanitation in Kumasi, Ghana: A contingent valuation study' in *Valuing Environmental Benefits in Developing Economies*, Michigan State University, Special Report no 29

Wilks, L C (1990) *A Survey of the Contingent Valuation Method* Resource Assessment Commission, RAC Research Paper no 2, Australian Government Publishing Service, Canberra

Williams, P H, Vane-Wright, R I and Humphries, C J (1991) 'Measuring Biodiversity for Choosing Conservation Areas' in LaSalle, J (ed) *Hymenoptera and Biodiversity* CAB International

Willis, K and Garrod, G (1991) 'Landscape Values: A Contingent Valuation Approach and Case Study of the Yorkshire Dales National Park' *Countryside Change Working Paper 21*, University of Newcastle upon Tyne

Willis, K (1993) *The National Oceanic and Atmospheric Administration Report on Contingent Valuation Methods: some comments* Department of Town and Country Planning, University of Newcastle upon Tyne (*mimeo*)

Wilson, E O (1988) 'The Current State of Biological Diversity' in Wilson, E O (ed) *Biodiversity* National Academy Press, Washington, pp 3–20

World Bank (1991) *World Tables 1991*, World Bank, Washington DC

A World Bank Operations Evaluation Study (1991) *Forestry: The World Bank's Experience*

World Resources Institute (1992) *World Resources 1992–1993*, Oxford University Press, Oxford

World Resources and International Institute for Environment and Development (1990) *World Resources 1990–1991* Earthscan, London

Wyman, R L (1990) 'What's happening to amphibians?' *Conservation Biology* 4, pp 350–352

INDEX

THE BLUEPRINT SERIES

BLUEPRINT FOR A GREEN ECONOMY
David Pearce, Anil Markandya and Edward B Barbier

Caused a huge impact on publication, and remains the most influential account available of the policies needed to achieve sustainability in a national economy. Widely adopted as a student textbook throughout the world.

'A political event of the first importance' – *The Guardian*

'Pearce's report may well be the beginning of an intellectual turnaround. His conclusions are necessarily controversial' – *The Daily Telegraph*

Paperback   £8.95   ISBN 1 85383 066 6   192 pages   1989

BLUEPRINT 2: GREENING THE WORLD'S ECONOMY
Edited by David Pearce

Extends the application of environmental economics to management of the global environment, providing an agenda for international and governmental action

'Admirably clear-headed in an area where muddle is often king ... an excellent introduction to the most pressing environmental issues' – *Financial Times*

Paperback   £9.95   ISBN 1 85383 076 3   224 pages   1991

BLUEPRINT 3: MEASURING SUSTAINABLE DEVELOPMENT
Published in association with CSERGE
David Pearce and others

After developing the policies necessary to achieve sustainability, Pearce continues his groundbreaking series by showing in a direct and non-technical way how to measure whether progress towards sustainable development is being made. His conclusions contrast sharply with the British Government's efforts to date.

Paperback   £10.95   ISBN 1 85383 183 2   176 pages   1994

BLUEPRINT 4: SUSTAINING THE EARTH
Capturing Global Value
Published in association with CSERGE and the ESRC
Edited by David Pearce

Looks at the opportunities for using markets forces to improve the global environment by trying to 'capture' the value of different environmental goods.

To be published in February 1995

Paperback   £10.95   ISBN 1 85383 184 0   192 pages

OTHER RELEVANT PUBLICATIONS

PARADISE LOST?
The Ecological Economies of Biodiversity
Published in association with the Beijer Institute
Edward B Barbier, Joanne C Burgess, Carl Folke

Loss of biodiversity – the variation within the living world essential for all life – ranges from the small scale breakdown of local ecosystems to species extinction at the extreme. Three leading enviro mental economists seek to remove the uncertainty and ignorance which underlies the biodiversity problem and demonstrate exactly what is at stake in one of the crucial issues confronting the world.

Paradise Lost? takes an integrated ecological and economic approach to the issue and looks at the causes of biodiversity loss. It analyses in detail key ecosystems, showing the effects such an approach would have in each, and examines how these lessons can be incorporated into conservation policy in the future.

Paperback   £13.95   ISBN 1 85383 181 6   350 pages

ECONOMIC VALUES AND THE NATURAL WORLD
David Pearce

David Pearce looks at one of the most important issues for economists in dealing with environmental problems: how to place economic values on our environment. He shows how the different methods have been applied in practice – with numerous case studies and analysis – and explains how the results provide an economic rationale for dealing with global environmental problems whether they be loss of biodiversity or atmospheric pollution.

'Everyone concerned with environmental degradation can be grateful to Pearce for stressing forcefully and effectively that the environment has considerable economic value which must somehow be taken into account if wealth creation is to be sustainable.' – *Resurgence*

Paperback   £10.95   ISBN 1 85383 152 2   144 pages

If you would like to order an Earthscan catalogue, or to receive more information about these or any other Earthscan publications, then please write to:

Earthscan Publications Ltd, 120 Pentonville Road, London N1 9JN
Tel: 071 278 0433   Fax: 071 278 1142